A complete, and as yet unrecognized change has taken place in the problems of ethics and morals. This occurred at 8:15 A.M. on August 6, 1945, when the first atomic bomb lit up the sky over Hiroshima. Up to that moment there had been two ways of designing an ethical system—two sets of reasons for making moral decisions.

The first set is that some things are considered to be good in themselves. One should feed the hungry, protect the weak and so forth. The Ten Commandments are widely believed to be good without further explanation—they should be obeyed because that is what a good person would do.

The second set were things that should be done because of how the results would affect you. In this set are beliefs (such as that of Plato) that leading a virtuous life would make you happier. Other beliefs of this sort would be that you should so act as to insure good Karma, or that you should act only for yourself as that is what everyone does and it is the only way to survive.

These two were the only bases for ethical beliefs and systems in the past. Neither of them has been very effective in preventing wars or in protecting the environment in which we live.

Now a third basis for morality exists. This rests on a purely human characteristic—the wish for the human race to continue to exist.

Today it is no longer only a problem of what a "good" person would do, or of what will happen to the individual or even to the specific society or culture. It is now a problem of the survival of the human race itself. This is one wish that all sane human beings agree on. The concept of a future without the existence of our species leads to the emptiness and meaninglessness of all our actions.

Since that morning at Hiroshima, our racial existence is threatened. A new moral imperative exists—that we so act as to make most likely the continued existence of our species. This book will explore the necessary change in ethics which is now necessary and its implications.

In the past, metaphysical and theological assumptions strongly influenced our views of ethics. The assumptions we made concerning the nature of the cosmos and the existence or nonexistence of God determined, at any rate, how we *ought* to behave. The point of view of this book is founded on psychological assumptions—the fact that human beings *desire* the continuation of our race and that this issue is now in doubt is our starting point. The nature of reality and the existence of God is seen as secondary.

AN ETHIC FOR
THE AGE OF SPACE

ALSO BY LAWRENCE LESHAN

The Psychosomatic Aspects of Neoplastic Disease
(coedited with David Kissen)

Counseling The Dying
(with Jackson, Bowers and Knight)

*You Can Fight For Your Life: Emotional Factors
in the Treatment of Cancer*

*The Mechanic and the Gardener: How to Use
the Holistic Revolution in Medicine*

Towards a General Theory of the Paranormal

The Medium, the Mystic and the Physicist

How to Meditate

Alternate Realities

Cancer as a Turning Point

Einstein's Space and Van Gogh's Sky
(with Henry Margeau)

The Science of the Paranormal: The Next Frontier

The Dilemma of Psychology

The Psychology of War

Beyond Technique: Psychotherapy for the 21st Century

An Ethic for the Age of Space

A Touchstone for Conduct Among the Stars

Lawrence LeShan, Ph. D.

SAMUEL WEISER, INC.

York Beach, Maine

First published in 1996
by Samuel Weiser, Inc.
P. O. Box 612
York Beach, ME 03910-0612

Library of Congress Cataloging-in-Publication Data
LeShan, Lawrence L., 1920-
   An ethic for the age of space/Lawrence LeShan.
      p.   cm.
   Includes bibliographical references.
   1. Ethics.   I. Title.
BJ1012.L46   1996
170—dc20

ISBN 0-87728-854-2   95-48385
CCP   CIP

Cover art is a watercolor titled "The Path II," by Rob Schouten.
Copyright © 1996 Rob Schouten.

Typeset in 10 point Century Light
Text Design by Leslie Carlson
Printed in the United States of America

04 03 02 01 00 99 98 97 96
10 9   8   7   6   5   4   3   2   1

The paper used in this publication meets the minimum requirements of the American National Standard for Permanence of
Paper for Printed Library Materials Z39.48–1984.

TABLE OF CONTENTS

PREFACE

The subject of this book has intrigued me since 1928 when I read my first copy of *Amazing Stories Magazine*. Since then I have been concerned with the problem of what conditions and what situations the human race would face as we moved forward in time and in technology and outward in space.

Seven years later I arrived at the New York Museum of Natural History at 7 A.M. one Saturday morning to be close to the head of the line that was already forming. By 10 A.M. when the museum opened, a large group of young people were waiting patiently to put down our dollar bills (a good sum in 1935: I earned mine by shoveling snow off the neighbors' walks and driveways the winter before at fifteen cents a house) to make a reservation for a seat on the first passenger liner to go to the Moon. We knew that there would be such a liner one day and believed firmly that it would be in our lifetime. I wonder now what ever became of that reservation book in which we so carefully printed our names and addresses. I must have been given a receipt, but I have no memory of receiving or having one. It was an exciting time—we believed in the future and that it would become better and better. There would be problems, yes, but human beings would solve them.

I personally must have learned this attitude from my father. He had wanted to become an engineer, but the necessity of having to help support his younger brothers and sisters through school forced him to give up his plans (except for an occasional night course at Cooper Union) and go into business. But his interest and orientation remained to the end of his life.

His last words before he died in 1929 were, "I wish I could live ten more years to see the wonderful things science will do."[1]

The rate of advancement in the physical sciences has indeed been wonderful. We have instruments that can see and photograph inside the human body without breaking the skin. We can view molecules with one instrument and distant galaxies with another. Great music, once played, is not lost forever, but can be recorded and replayed indefinitely. Our words and pictures flash across the world even faster than our bodies are transported through the skies. We can replace diseased hearts and kidneys and could, if we wished, completely wipe out the great killers of the past—cholera, black plague, and other such diseases. (We could feed the world from the Midwest of the United States and clothe it from its South.) What would have seemed like sorcery at one time is understood by most school children 30 years later.

Each advance in our ability to control matter and energy, however, has brought new and unforeseen problems with it. We have polluted whole areas of our lovely world; are poisoning the oceans on which our supply of oxygen largely depends; our inner cities are sewers in which millions must live; our advances in medical technology have been accompanied by a loss of humanity in most of our medical establishments; Chernobyl-like incidents or worse, spewing their 10,000-year deaths into the air, will certainly be increasingly frequent as more and more atomic plants all over the world go into operation. Our population increases with no end in sight. Advertising agencies use modern communication equipment to get better *images* elected to high office, not better people. Computers bring new types

---

[1] My brother and sister, both long dead now, also became involved in science. She wanted to become a physician, but medical school quotas on gender and religion prevailed even over her Phi Beta Kappa grades and prevented this. My brother became a nuclear physicist.

of crime into being as well as new ways of destroying privacy, and the horrors of war get greater and greater. By pressing a button, one person can destroy a city and then, by the reaction of others, the whole human race. In the halcyon days of science fiction in my youth, as we peered into the future, we saw little of this. With optimistic eyes, we saw the benefits of new technology in the physical sciences and the possibility of new adventures, not the negatives that have accompanied it.

We have made great and almost unbelievable progress in the last three centuries, in physics, chemistry, in the arts, and in all the sciences except one—we have not learned how to live better with each other and with the general nature of which we all are a part. The science of human consciousness and behavior has been a dismal failure. The information and technology explosions have changed everything about the way we live except the ways we interact with each other and with the ecology. Indeed, as far as the ecology goes, our new technology has made things far worse. The Roman Empire at its height, for example, simply did not have the ability to destroy the oxygen-producing function of the oceans or to cut down the rain forests. We do have this ability and are doing these things! In the words of Konrad Lorenz:

> Now, as never before, the prospects for a human future are exceptionally dismal. Most probably the human race will soon end swiftly, but certainly not painlessly, through use of extant nuclear weapons. Even if this does not happen, every human being remains in peril through poisoning and desiccating the environment in which he lives and by which he is sustained.[2]

I have written elsewhere why I believe that psychology has failed

---

[2] Konrad Lorenz, *The Waning of Humanness* (Boston: Little Brown, 1983), unpaged foreword.

as a science.[3] This book, however, has a larger question. In the science fiction of my youth, as well as in the occasional science fiction stories I read today, human beings, tapping the power of the atom, traveling in space ships through the solar system and far beyond, act toward each other and toward nature pretty much like the people I saw around me and the people I read about in H. G. Wells' *Outline of History* (a favorite and much studied book of both my father and myself as a child) and in other history books. I wondered then—as I have ever since— why this is so and what are the implications of it for the future.

Many years later, I found that Arthur Koestler had reached the same conclusions and had expressed them far better than I could.

> The heroes of science-fiction have unlimited power and fantastic possibilities, but their feelings and thoughts are limited within the narrow human range. Tom Corbett, Space Cadet, behaves the same way on the third planet of Orion as he does in a drugstore in Minnesota. The Milky Way has simply become an extension of Main Street.[4]

This wonderment played a large part in my choosing psychology as my profession. Here, I hoped, in the science of human consciousness and behavior, I would find the answers. Alas! they were not there, but I learned from my teachers new ways to think about the problem.

For a long time we human beings could "get away" with continuing the old patterns of behavior. This is no longer true. Since the 6th of August, 1945, when the atom bomb was dropped for the first time on living human beings, our old pat-

---

[3] L. LeShan, *The Dilemma of Psychology: A Psychologist Looks at His Troubled Profession* (New York: Dutton, 1990).

[4] Arthur Koestler, *The Trail of the Dinosaur* (New York: Macmillan, 1955), p. 147.

terns of behavior lead to racial suicide. We all know this, but we seem unable to change.

This book will show that no matter what happens in the next period—the age of atomics and of space—if we continue to behave as we have in the past, we will almost certainly be exterminated. And after over sixty years of involvement with the problem, it is increasingly clear to me that we have not changed in meaningful ways in the past and are not likely to do so in the future.

This book concerns one crucial aspect of our inability to change: the ethical guidelines which determine how we react in different situations: not the guidelines we profess, but those we actually use. These range from "Every man for himself" to "Women and children to the lifeboats first" (see the Titanic experience for a good example of this), and to the Golden Rule. The guidelines we have do not, however, generally serve to keep us from continuing to kill each other. (In the first twenty years after World War II there were, according to Adlai Stevenson, more than twenty wars in which national armies fought armed battles.) Further, there is widespread awareness today of how rapidly we are destroying the ecology on which we depend for air, water, and food, and yet we can no more seem to stop it than we can arrest our insane population growth.

The need for a new overall ethical guideline has become even greater as the pace of social change—and with it our accustomed guidelines and anchors to reality—increases as it has done in the past one hundred and fifty years. Whether this pace will continue to accelerate is impossible to say, but for the past century and a half it has been extremely rapid when we compare to the previous life of the human race. And so far it has continued to get more rapid.

In 1815, 99 percent of the human race had no light at night except from fireplaces and bound bundles of burning reeds.

XII AN ETHIC FOR THE AGE OF SPACE

Just as in the Stone Age, night darkness was almost complete from dusk to dawn. By 1915 the streets and houses in Western Europe and the United States were lit by gas and electricity. The hours of leisure and of creativity were enormously increased. We changed more in one hundred years than in the previous 50,000.

The Nobel Laureate Albert Szent-Georgyi has put it thusly:

... in this century we have increased our speed of communication by a factor of 10^7 (ten million fold), our speed of travel by a factor of 10^2, our speed of data handling by 10^6, our energy resources by 10^3, our ability to control disease by something like 10^2, and the rate of population growth to 10^3 times what it was a few thousand years ago. [5]

Norman Cantor adds:

All through the 19th century there was an enormous expansion of literacy and knowledge and a concomitant increase in ideological commitment. The historical timetable accelerated in unprecedented ways and the clock of human events moved at breakneck speed in comparison to the pre-industrial world.[6]

In the thirty years following World War II, television spread all over the Western world and completely changed our relations to events outside of our local area and to our governments. We saw everything that was going on as it happened. No longer, for example, is a United States president a woodcut, a slogan, a report in a newspaper, a photograph, or even a voice on the

---

[5] Albert Szent-Gyorgyi, *The Crazy Ape* (New York: Philosophical Library, 1970), p. 16.

[6] Norman Cantor and Michael Wertheimer, *The Making of the Modern World, 1815-1914* (New York: Thomas Crowell, 1967), p. 2.

radio. He is there in the flesh, present for all of us. The implications of this change are not yet clear except that they are very
large for our view of ourselves and the world, and therefore
our ethical systems which depend on this to a large extent.

When I think back on the changes that have occurred even
in my own lifespan, I become even more conscious of the ra-
pidity of this change and how it affects my view of reality. In
my youth we had a radio, but in order to listen to a half-hour
program, we first had to charge the battery for an hour. (There
was only one program widely listened to—"The Happiness
Boys"—a half hour on Wednesday evenings and my father would
arrive home early those nights to make sure that the radio was
properly charging.) You could hear good music at home, but
you wound the victrola by hand for each record. Airplane travel
was almost as unheard of as television. Automobile speeds were
limited to 25 or 30 miles an hour, and in an afternoon's outing
you reasonably expected at least one blowout. Every 10-year-
old knew how to change a tire and repair the inner tube. The
changes in our social life since then due to the rapid growth
and availability of technology have been much larger than we
are usually conscious of. If only in our greater mobility we became so much more free. It has been largely remarked among
sociologists (I do not know who first made this observation)
that Henry Ford brought together the automobile and the assembly line and thereby changed the sex habits of the United
States. There is more to this concept than we usually are aware.

In 1980, personal computers were a rarity and found mainly
on the desks of scientists. By 1990 they were widely found in
the possession of schoolchildren, housewives, and in just about
every other segment of society.

An ethical system rests on what our society has taught us
about what we and the world are. We need an ethical directive
that will fit with the rapidly changing times we live in: one that

AN ETHIC FOR THE AGE OF SPACE

rests on an axiom we can depend on to remain vital in an unpredictable future.

This book will explore our old guidelines for our behavior and their overall failure. It will then discuss one very widespread idea and belief that makes new and positive change so incredibly difficult. From there it will go to a new concept of science developed at the turn of the century contradicting this idea and how this new concept leads to a new ethical guideline, which can help us survive on either this planet alone or also on others.

The other aspects of this new ethical guideline will then be explored. First how we can use it to lessen the misunderstandings with others, and second, when it is inapplicable. The last part of the book will describe an educational system which can help us survive in the next period of human history.

This book is the summing up of a lifelong quest: What is most likely to happen in this new age brought to us by science?

How can we best prepare for the new age which is clearly here? Everything has changed except our behavior. If we do not change that we will die as a race. I have been concerned with this problem for more than half a century. I have seen and been fascinated by "the wonderful things science has done" in the interim. It is with gratitude for this concern and fascination that this book is dedicated to my father,

Julius LeShan.

Acknowledgments

I would like to express my appreciation to the staff of the Centerville Library on Cape Cod and to the staff of the Fordham University Library at Lincoln Center. Without their help and assistance this book could not have been written.

And to Eda LeShan, who made major contributions to this work, particularly in those chapters on the education of children, my gratitude and love.

The quotes that appear at the chapter openings come from the following sources:

Page 1: Oliver Wendall Holmes, quoted in Gardner Murphy, *Human Potentialities* (New York: Basic Books, 1958), p. vi.

Page 19: George Bernard Shaw, *Caesar and Cleopatra*, Act 3.

Page 29: Albert Einstein and Leopold Infeld, *The Evolution of Physics* (New York: Simon & Schuster, 1961), p. 33.

Page 43: William James, *Principles of Psychology* (New York: Dover; reprint of 1890 text).

Page 63: Bertand Russell, *Unpopular Essays* (New York: Simon & Schuster, 1950), p. 155.

Page 75: Pascal, *Pensées* (London: J. M. Dent, 1932), p. 44.

Page 97: Thomas Hood, quoted in Ernst Becker, *Escape From Evil* (New York: Free Press, 1875).

Page 109: H. G. Wells, quoted in H. J. Bridges, ed., *Aspects of Ethical Religion* (New York: American Ethical Union, 1926), p. 47.

Page 119: Jacob Needleman, *The Heart of Philosophy* (New York: Knopf, 1982), p. 49.

At the beginning of this epoch God handed man the atomic bomb, saying: "Here, either learn to live together or finish the entire thing and I'll start over."

—United States Vice-President Henry Wallace

CHAPTER ONE

THE PROBLEM OF ETHICS IN THE AGE OF SPACE

I think it is not improbable that man, like the grub that prepares a chamber for the winged thing it has never seen but is to be—that man may have cosmic destinies that he does not understand. And so beyond the vision of battling races and impoverished earth I catch a dreaming glimpse of peace.

—Oliver Wendall Holmes

A new age is here and we, willing or unwilling, hopeful or despairing, are living during its birthing and its terrible birth pangs. All over the world the giant nuclear plants rear their squat towers into the air and remind us of what nuclear leakage or meltdown can do to the county, country, continent, and planet. Arsenals of atomic bombs, each capable of destroying a city, together capable of destroying the life-sustaining qualities of Earth, are held by more and more nations each decade.

Human beings have crossed space and walked on our nearest solar neighbor, and our instrument packages fly close to the once unimaginably distant other planets, from burning Venus to frigid Pluto. The science fiction dreams of my youth seem everyday more antique, naive, and outmoded.

Our physical technology increases daily at such a rate that it is almost impossible for specialists to keep up with more than one narrow field of science. Our computers grow more complex and can do more every year. We are just beginning to realize how different our world is from the one we lived in during the first half of this century and all the centuries before. We are also just beginning to realize the dangers we are in as a species due to the new technology. With this realization is coming a new awareness that the human race must change its age-old patterns of behavior if it is likely to survive for very long. Even before the development of the atomic bomb, some far-seeing thinkers looked ahead and saw the point to which the increasing difference between social and technological development was bringing us. Freud wrote in 1929 in his *Civilization and Its Discontents:*

> The fateful question for the human species seems to me to be whether and to what extent their cultural development will succeed in mastering the disturbance of their communal life by the human instinct of aggression and self destruction....Men have gained control over the forces of nature to such an extent that with their help they would have no difficulty in exterminating one another to the last man.[1]

In 1916, Wilfred Trotter wrote in his classic *The Herd Instinct:*

> ...it needs but little imagination to see that the probabilities are very great that after all man will prove to

---

[1] Sigmund Freud, *Civilization and its Discontent* (New York: W.W.Norton & Co., 1962).

be one more of Nature's failures ignominiously swept
from her work-table to make way for another venture
of her tireless curiosity and patience.[2]

Our patterns of behavior are determined, in large part, by our
systems of making choices—the ethical guidelines we use. The
purpose of this book is to help us develop ethical guidelines
that may enable us to survive in the next period of human existence.

A birthing time is a time of new opportunities and great
dangers. To the degree we are aware of them, we can grasp the
one and avoid the other. Socrates, who, to our knowledge, first
started the serious study of the problem of ethics, said that his
mother was a midwife. I hope that this book will serve in the
same way as does that ancient and honorable profession, to
help the healthy birthing of a new age so that we may survive
in the strange and frightening period into which we, willing or
no, are moving.

As we move into the age of space there are a vast number of
specific possibilities as to what may happen in the future, but
only a limited number of general ones.

1. We do not find other habitable-for-human planets

2. We find other habitable-for-human planets

3. We do not encounter other sapient races

4. We encounter other sapient races

These are, of course, not absolute. We may not find other habitable-for-humans planets and yet build colonies in space in
artificial constructions. We may meet sapient species whose
kind of intelligence is so far from ours that we do not recognize

---

[2] Quoted in David Muzzey, "The Ethical Impact of History," in H.J. Bridges,
Aspects of Ethical Religion (New York: American *Ethical Union,* 1926),
p. 48.

it. If we find other habitable-for-humans planets they may or may not be inhabited by other sentient species. Other possibilities may develop. But, by and large, these are the general possibilities which exist and for which we must plan.

If we members of the human race behave in the future as we have behaved in the past, there is an overwhelming probability that we will be destroyed no matter which of the four general possibilities actually occurs. Let us briefly examine each of these.

1. We do not find other habitable planets and continue the same patterns of behavior.

We are poisoning the Earth and rapidly overpopulating it. The forests and seas are being destroyed and our environmental protection is moving toward collapse. The technology we use to do this, as well as the population using this technology, is constantly and rapidly increasing. Continuing our present patterns of behavior, we will certainly destroy ourselves by poisoning and overpopulating our only planet.[3]

The second pattern of behavior which human beings have consistently followed all through our recorded history is war. Unless we change this pattern, war will eventually take place between countries having both atomic weapons and delivery systems. (The number of these countries is steadily increasing.) On our track record, the losing country will, in spite of any promises or treaties to the contrary, almost certainly unleash these weapons. Whatever life will survive will not be human as we know it.

---

[3] "The ecological facts of life are grim. The survival of all living things—including man—is dependent on the integrity of the complex web of biological processes which comprise the earth's ecosystem. However, what man is now doing on the earth violates the fundamental requisites of man's existence...with tragic perversity we have linked much of our productive economy to precisely those features of technology which are ecologically destructive." Barry Commoner, "The Ecological Facts of Life," in Robert Disch, ed., *The Ecological Conscience* (Englewood Cliffs, N.J.: PrenticeHall, 1970), p. 2.

2. We do find other habitable-for-humans planets and continue the same patterns of behavior.

Modern technology has furthered tremendously our ability to both increase our population and to destroy the ecology on which our life depends. If we continue our past pattern of behavior, we will destroy the ability to support human life of any new planets which we settle. And we will do this far faster than we have done on our own home world. No matter how rapid are any interstellar transportation systems we devise and how many habitable planets we discover, the end will differ only in how long this takes.[4] Further, the technology necessary to settle new planets is very probably going to give us the technical ability necessary to wage interplanetary war. There is no reason to suppose we will stop this historically consistent pattern of behavior. So far we have seen no sign of a relationship between technological development and increasingly peaceful relationships between political entities.

3. We do not encounter other sapient races and continue the same patterns of behavior.

This reduces us to the possibilities of Numbers 1 and 2 and the overwhelming probability of our self-destruction.

4. We encounter other sapient races and continue the same patterns of behavior.

We have always made small or large differences between human groups the basis or excuse for war between them. Although we have not, to my knowledge, fought wars over which end of a boiled egg to open (as Dean Swift suggested in *Gulliver's Travels*), we have fought wars over just about every other

---

[4] There are limits on moving outward in space due to the relation between the volume and surface of a sphere. As the sphere increases in size, the volume increases more rapidly than the surface. The rate of possible escape from the sphere decreases as its size increases.

difference in opinion or in physical structure. Thus the question of whether the Holy Trinity was one in three or three in one has seemed to many to be a sufficient reason to engage in mutual slaughter. Color of skin, slant of eyes, possession of trade routes, States' rights versus Federal rights, loyalty to York or to Lancaster, or to North or South Korea, the right to sell opium to someone else's citizens, all served as excuses for discrimination, persecution, killing. The question of when the last holy appointee of God appeared on Earth has given Christians an excuse for persecuting Jews, and Mohammedans for persecuting Christians. Whatever the basic cause or causes of war, human beings have repeatedly and constantly engaged in it with great enthusiasm. Any differences, however small, have served as justification.

If we meet other sapient races, there will certainly be at least as large differences between humans and them as there are between various groups of humans. If we continue our previous and present patterns of behavior, we will certainly seize on these differences to express whatever drives us to war with our fellow humans.

Further, if we do meet other races of sapients, it is extremely likely that at least some of them will be more technologically and or militarily advanced than we are. Warfare at our present level of technology is clearly capable of exterminating our species. Warfare between races capable of interstellar flight will certainly have even greater capacity to do this.

With the tremendous and almost unimaginable number of stars in our galaxy alone, it is quite unlikely that if there are other sapient races, there is only one of them. We may subjugate or destroy any number of other sapient races. Sooner or later, however, the statistical probability is overwhelming that if there are other sapient races out there, we will meet one that can destroy us.

Our general patterns of behavior, such as wars, persecution of other groups who are different from us in some way, and a basic disdain for our ecological support system have been unchanged during recorded history. The industrial and information revolutions have changed everything in the way we live and in our ability to deal with matter and energy, but have not changed the mainsprings of human behavior. In addition, some beliefs have had, and still have, a sacred quality that most governments do not dare to touch, and those governments that have tried to deal with them have failed. These beliefs, which may have had survival value in the past, now lead to racial suicide. They include the "right" of every couple and every woman to have as many children as they wish or as impulse leads them to have. It also involves the "right" of every person to own as much physical property as they can accumulate, including, today, one or more automobiles. In a time of unchecked and rapid population growth, these beliefs can only lead to disaster on a global scale.

Curiously enough, the mental health movement in Western society during the last three quarters of the 20th century has had little effect on the development of ethical theory. This fact seems to stem from two sources. First, because the social sciences, including psychiatry, tried to model themselves on the "hard" sciences of the late 19th century, and to be as free of values as they could manage to be. That they were deluding themselves is now clear—a value-free psychotherapy, for example, is a contradiction in terms. Who could believe that the attitudes of a psychotherapist toward slavery, relations between the sexes, and so forth would not strongly influence his or her responses? But they believed that they were value-free and this "ethical relativism" (an ethical system in itself, although most psychotherapists were unaware of this) kept them from having a major influence on ethical concepts and beliefs.

The second major source of this lack of effect was the fact that definitions of mental health in a very general way always rested on the two objectives of minimized psychological distress and maximum effectiveness in interpersonal relationships. Whatever the formal definitions were, these two were almost invariably entailed. This led to strange and confused thinking. Who, for example, is the more mentally healthy—the often mentally distressed artist struggling painfully for a vision and a perfection he or she only dimly perceives, or the expertly manipulative psychopath who is very good indeed at interpersonal relationships, and who has very little if any mental pain? Or, to bring in another class, the chameleon of the "other-directed personality" who pleasantly, easily, and without inner conflict conforms to the views and beliefs of whatever group in which he finds himself.

These two ideals for which the various enterprises in mental health have striven arose from the medical model which this field placed in the seat of honor—the model to be emulated. It is in these two areas—mental distress and interpersonal relationships—that we most easily define "symptoms." Since the medical model states that the absence of symptoms equals health, it seemed naturally to follow that the absence of mental symptoms equals mental health.

Although the analogy of psychology to medicine was, and is, far from adequate, it has proven to be extremely durable. After psychology's long attempt to emulate physics had failed —after a hundred years of labor the mountain had barely produced a mouse—psychology turned to medicine as the successful and prestigious field on which to model itself. Little has come out of this, but in spite of many of our best pointing out the problem, the imitation seems to keep going on. When it threw out values and ethics, psychology and psychiatry so damaged themselves that they have only limped along ever since.

There have been a number of ethical guidelines, mandates for behavior, which the human race has traditionally used. None of these general rules for determining how we should act and react in any situation has demonstrated effectiveness in directing human behavior in such a way that we can reasonably expect to survive as a species in the coming age of space.[5] These include the following seven classes:

1. It is every man for himself and Heaven help the hindmost.
2. My brother and I against my cousin; my brother, my cousin and I against the world.
3. There is no meaning in ethics; they are an artifact of local cultural conditions and have no meaning beyond this.
4. Do unto others as you would be done by.
5. Your friends and neighbors may not be watching, but the Gods are. And they will judge you.
6. Act in such a way that if everyone did the same it would be a world in which you would like to live.
7. Live your life in harmony with the universe. This includes co-operating with perceptions of inevitable and predictable historical events. It also includes the belief that the customs of the culture in which you were raised are the "correct" and "right" customs.

---

[5] There are a number of widely reported objections to any ethical theory. Chief among these is the "self-evident" theory—belief that people will cheat or steal or do anything they perceive to be to their own advantage. The only reasons for not doing these things, says the belief, is fear of punishment or because of feeling superior to other people for not lying, cheating, etc. (This, of course, implies that all human beings are psychopaths and either cowards or prigs.) The evidence from history against this belief is so extensive that it is unnecessary to detail it here.

Whether or not the first of these guidelines "Every man for himself," with its consequent "Might makes right" is "realistic" or "valid" (whatever that means):

> ...it is incapable of furthering the most liveable life: for its very genius is to constrict, not enlarge, apprecia-tion of values. Wherever it rules it paralyzes social *imagination,* intensifies and spreads a destructive spirit, poisons the atmosphere with hatred and suspi-cion, and consequently is not directed toward but away from the attainment of the general welfare.[6]

In short, this ethical mandate is one that can only make the old patterns of behavior more prevailing and inescapable. It is pre-cisely these patterns which are intensified by this ethical guide-line which make most likely the eradication of the human species.

The second mandate—"My group against all others," is very widespread. In Albert Schweitzer's words:

> For the primitive the circle of solidarity is restricted. It is limited...to the members of his tribe which he re-gards as a larger family....In my hospital I have primi-tives. When I have occasion to ask a patient of this category to render some small service to a bedridden fellow-patient, he will oblige only if the latter belongs to his tribe. If this is not the case, he will reply quite candidly 'This is not brother for me.' No amount of per-suasion and no kind of threat will budge him from his refusal to do the unimaginable thing: putting himself out for a stranger. I am the one who has to give in.[7]

---

[6] Max Otto, *Science and the Moral Life* (New York: Mentor-NAL, 1949), p. 63.

[7] Albert Schweitzer, "The Problem of Ethics for Twentieth-Century Man," in *The Saturday Review of Literature,* 13 June 1953.

U.S. Chief Justice Earl Warren wrote:

> If he [Cain] had slain the member of another family, or
> clan, or tribe [depending on the degree of civilization],
> he would not have been punished, and his deed would
> not have been considered wrong by his relatives or
> clansmen or tribesmen. Law and ethics, which in primi-
> tive life are identical, protected only those within a lim-
> ited group. In general they offered little protection to
> outsiders.[8]

Pascal wrote in this context:

> "What do you gain by slaying me? I am unarmed." What!
> do you not live across the water? If you lived on this
> side, my friend, I should be a murderer and it would be
> wrong thus to kill you; but since you live on the other
> side I am a hero and am doing the right thing.[9]

The popular classical Greek morality, "Do harm to your enemies
and good to your friends" grew out of the second ethical mandate, "My brother and I...." This mandate is related to various
versions of "The Chosen People" concept. This ranges from
the ancient Hebrew tribes to various primitive groups in which
the name of the group and the term "Human Being" are defined as the same thing, to the citizens of classical Athens (they
defined other humans as "barbarians") to the Aryan idiocy and
tragedy of 20th-century Germany, to South African and United
States white supremacist groups, and to innumerable other
versions of "We are the real people—all others are below us."
The logical consequence of moral provincialism is the view that
moral principles apply only to problems involving intra-group

---

[8] Earl G. Warren, "The Law Beyond the Law," in *Main Currents in Modern Thought.* Retrospective Issue, Nov. 17, 1975 (163-168), Vol. 32, p.
163.
[9] Blaise Pascal, *Pensées* (London: J. M. Dent, 1932), p. 79.

relations. Problems of intertribal, or interracial or international or intercultural or interspecies relations are either to be solved by force or not to be solved at all.

The third guideline (ethics are local cultural artifacts) leads to the first two. It offers no other guidelines for behavior. This view, brought into prominence again by Marxism and by modern anthropology, was first raised by the Greek thinkers after Protagoras. They felt that all morals were conventions and had nothing to do with the basic nature of reality. Some believed that morals were designed by the weak and many to prevent the few and powerful from getting the better of them. Some believed the reverse, that morals were made by the rich and powerful to protect their privileges. A more modern version attributes all morals to psychological structure. Usually these are construed to be either pathological drives within the individual or to defenses against these drives. A recent psychology textbook states, "Values and meanings are nothing but defense mechanisms and reaction formations."[10]

The 7th guideline "Live your life in harmony with the universe" has led, in the past, to a great deal of conflict as the perception of what the universe is about varies so much with different groups. "Both sides," said Abraham Lincoln in 1862, "believe that they are acting in accord with the will of God." As an ethical principle it fills people with good feeling, but has not seemed to be at all useful in leading to peace nor to the protection of the ecology of the planet. The trouble with using, as a basis for morality, "the way the universe works, or "Natural Law" or the "Law of Nature" or concepts of this sort, is that it can—like scripture—be quoted for any purpose. The legal theorist Edmund Cahn says that when applied to law:

> ...lawyers and judges could quote the vague maxim of the law of nature for any purpose whatever, for revolu-

---

[10] Quoted by Arthur Koestler in *Janus* (New York: Random House, 1978).

tion and reaction, plutocracy and community of goods. Natural Law might be nailed to anyone's mast. It was fact, so universal that it could never be found. [11]

The most usual form of Number 7 ("Live your life in harmony with the universe") is following the ethics of custom. Tradition, convention, and custom mark the difference between right and wrong. What is customary and legal is right simply because it is the custom or the law. The "view of the world I grew up with" and the actions implied by this, are seen as in conformance with natural law and reflecting it. Simply put, the most widely accepted principle in ethics is the principle that the ways I was taught to behave as a child are the correct ways, and anyone who does not follow them is a bad person. Einstein once defined "common sense" as "that collection of prejudices you accumulated by age 18."[12] It would be correct to state that most people's belief in what is moral also fits this definition. Since, however, what is taught to children about morality in one culture often differs very much from that taught in neighboring ones, this cannot lead to peaceful relationships.

These seven positions are oversimplified for the sake of clarity and discussion. In reality there are other coherent ethical viewpoints, but these seven cover the general ground of these moral positions by which people live, and for which they fight and sometimes die. From the viewpoint of this book, we are dealing with a well-observed fact as the basis of an ethical system. This is a psychological fact and clear observation. Therefore we do not need the appeal to supernatural authority of some systems, or a basis in metaphysical concept of reality on which others depend, nor the elaborate grammatical analyses of

---

[11] Edmund Cahn, *The Sense of Injustice* (London: Oxford University Press, 1949), p. 7.

[12] Albert Einstein, quoted in Susanne Langer, "On Cassirer's Theory of Language to Myth," in P.A. Schilpp, ed., *The Philosophy of Ernst Cassirer* (Evanston, IL: Library of Living Philosophers, 1949), p. 381.

much of modern philosophy. It is a fact that we deeply wish the human race to continue to exist, and that the opposite would make our lives and activities seem meaningless to us. This is a human imperative and call to action and we are human. The elaborations of the philosophers who have studied ethics—their categories such as "ethical idealism," "libertarianism," "ethical formalism," "egoistic hedonism," and so forth, become pale and empty compared to the deep tide of the racial threat we now face. They are ripples on the water on the beach as the tidal wave threatens to sweep in from offshore.

All people follow some ethical rule, although it may not be the one they profess, the one they admire, or the one which they believe themselves to follow. A person may advance and claim (to self as well as to others) that he or she is following a "Golden Rule" standard of ethics, when in actuality the person is following a "me-first" and expediency rule (ethical rules are local artifacts and have no real validity) of morality.

Even when we profess belief in an ethical mandate and believe that we believe in it, we frequently do not follow it in our daily life and activity. "This" situation seems different to us, and we behave far differently than we have preached to others and to ourselves as to how we "should" act. In Ovid's words:

> I hear desire say "yes" and reason "no" and see with open eyes the better cause, and know it is better, yet I pursue the worse. [13]

Or, as St. Paul put it: "For the good that I would I do not do, but the evil which I would not, that I do."[14] However, whether it is the one they profess or not, all human beings follow an ethical code.

---

[13] Ovid, *Metamorphosis,* 4–18.
[14] St. Paul, Romans 7:19.

It is very likely that if the 4th ethical mandate ("Do Unto Others"), 5th ("The gods are watching or—You are affecting your karma), or 6th ("What would happen if everyone did that?") had ever been followed by a majority of our species, our human condition would be so much better that we might hope to survive among the stars. However, they have not been followed except by individuals and small groups. I am reminded of the time Mahatma Gandhi was asked what he thought of Western civilization. He replied, "I think it would be a fine idea."

Whatever the reasons these three ethical mandates have had no major effect on our behavior, it is clear that they have not. Advanced over and over again in many different ways by our spiritual and intellectual leaders, they have often received lip service by the many, been obeyed by a few, and never prevented a war, or the use of a new weapon, or kept us from poisoning our environment. No matter how strong the emotional attachment we have to one or another of them, no matter how much we feel it should work and positively affect our species, the fact remains that these mandates have failed us. As a species we do not act in terms of them. Our patterns of behavior are not determined by them and many of these patterns are anti-survival. Since the new age began on August 6, 1945 at the death of Hiroshima, and began adolescence on July 20, 1969 when Neil Armstrong first stepped on the Moon, our old patterns lead to the overwhelming probability of the death of all our grandchildren or great-grandchildren. Unless we, or some other race, fragmentize our planet or nova our Sun, traces of our works—pyramids and superhighways—will outlast human life. A new ethical guideline, a new mandate for behavior, is clearly and desperately needed. There are certain requirements the new mandate must fulfill if it is to be useful in the new age into which we humans are moving. These are:

1. It must be in accord with the philosophy and underlying principles of modern science. We are, for better or worse, a society which believes that real answers to our problems come only from science and that any statement contradicting or irrelevant to the scientific approach is invalid. [15]

2. It must be general enough so that it covers the vast array of possible situations that will arise as we move out into space. It also, however, must be specific enough that it can be used as a guide to behavior in concrete and actual situations.

3. It must respect the right to be different in physical structure, ideas, ways of organizing reality, beliefs and behavior, whether these differences are exhibited and acted upon by other humans or by non-human sapients.

4. Although this respect must be a central tenet, it must also protect the individual using it, human children[16] and the human race generally.

Ethics necessarily includes the concept of "should," what the individual "should" do in various circumstances. This concept, however, consists of two very separate meanings. The first is, "You should do so-and-so because a 'good' person would do it," or "It is good in itself to do thus-and-so (e.g., feed the hungry) and therefore you should do it." It is this kind of ethical statement and argument that has made our ethical theory appear to be outmoded and so little regarded in our present day. Our late

---

[15] "...science and the machine are two inevitable facts with which all must reckon who write, teach, preach, lead and practice the arts in our time. Those who refuse to face them are condemned in advance to sterility and defeat." Charles Beard, *Whither Mankind* (New York: Lomgmans-Green, 1928), p. 19. Since Beard wrote these words, they have become far more obvious and clear. Every decade since, science has taken on more authority and more and more complex definitions of "machine" are widely used.

[16] The first business of any species is to protect and rear its young. When it fails at this, the species dies.

20th-century view of reality simply does not see the universe as committed to prefer any one ethical system.

The other meaning is that if you want to accomplish a specific thing, (i.e, go to Chicago), you should do so-and-so (i.e., buy an airplane ticket, or a train ticket, or get a good pair of shoes). You should do something because it is a necessary part of the path to accomplishing something you wish. If you want to avoid being run over in the traffic, you should look both ways at the street corner.

In any serious human matter, we must ask a basic question. The philosopher Max Otto has put it: "The deepest source of a man's philosophy, the one that shapes and nourishes it, is faith or lack of faith in mankind."[17] (Today we would say "humankind" but the statement is the same.) In this area our confusion in the last half of the 20th century has passed all bounds of the ancient world and the past. We no longer believe that we are the children of God, or made in the image of God, but instead believe we are the offspring of animals. And—as the descendents of apes—our only hope is progress. But we no longer believe in progress.

We have given up hope that religion, social change, education, or political systems will save us. The question is no longer of our belief in God, but our belief in the human race. The question is no longer that of the individual surviving death, but of humanity surviving its own accomplishments.

It was the philosopher René Descartes in the 17th century who first formed the idea of finding a single, not open-to-doubt axiom, and building an entire philosophical system of this unshakeable base. This was the reason he selected his famous "I think therefore I am." He believed that he could, from this, develop a complete picture of reality so that the physical world,

---

[17] Max Otto, *Science and the Moral Life*, p. 27.

at least, could be understood in its entirety and its actions predicted.

He failed in this magnificent essay and I am not trying here to repeat his attempt. I do not believe that even the physical world will ever be completely predictable (quantum mechanics has demonstrated the impossibility of this for the realm of the very small). Further, it seems inconceivable to me that the mental and behavioral world of human individuals will ever be predictable. In addition, many moral judgements will frequently have a gray area around them blurring the absolute right and wrong. (Some will not. The religious leader John Lovejoy Elliot, speaking of the German concentration camps, said "I am not an absolutist, but some things are absolutely wrong."[18])

However, with these limitations, a general ethical directive, like that presented in this book, can be useful in helping us guide our behavior. Furthermore, it is built on a solid axiom: that we are human beings and, therefore, wish the human race to continue to exist. Whoever doubts the axiom, like the person who is not enraged when a child is being beaten, has given up his or her claim to be human.

Before we can talk about the specifics of the new mandate, it is necessary to look at some background material.

---

[18] John Lovejoy Elliot, from a lecture given to the Ethical Culture Society, New York City, 1940.

CHAPTER TWO

THE DEADLIEST IDEA HUMAN BEINGS HAVE EVER DEVELOPED

Britannicus (shocked): Caesar, this is not proper.

Theodotus (outraged): How?

Caesar (recovering his self-possession): Pardon him, Theodotus. He is a barbarian and thinks that the customs of his tribe and island are the laws of nature.

—George Bernard Shaw

There has been one idea nearly ubiquitous in human thought, that has made it almost impossible for different groups of human beings to live together in harmony. It will certainly continue to exert its overwhelming influence toward intergroup conflict if we meet other sapient species. We see this idea underlying the work of Classical authors, Russian novelists, Eastern "wisdom" seekers and almost anywhere else we care to look. It is agreed on by the sages of Greece, the ancient manuscripts of Hinduism, the prophets of Israel, the arhats of

Buddhism, the saints of Christianity, and most of the philosophers whose works are taught in our universities. This idea has
three parts.

1. Any genuine question must have one and only one true
   answer. All other answers are necessarily errors.
2. There is one and only one dependable path toward the discovery of this truth.[1]
3. The true answer, when found, must necessarily be compatible
   with all other truths and form a single whole. One truth
   cannot be incompatible with another.[2]

We believe this three-part truth to be true a priori.

This is a basic faith of nearly all human cultures. We imbibe it
with our mother's milk and feel that to question it is a mark of
insanity.

The few serious attacks on this idea in the past have been
relegated to the dustbin of discarded ideas. These include
Aristotle's concept of different laws governing earthly and heavenly events, and the views of Averroes, and of Siger, of Brabant,
that reason and revelation could lead to very different but

---

[1] Socrates saw logic and intellectual clarity as the path to this one truth.
Others have seen as correct revelation, the ways of our ancestors, scripture from the Bible, the philosophy in *Das Kapital*, drugs, dreams,
transcendance, and a wide variety of other paths. Most simply take the
accepted wisdom of their subculture as the guide to truth.

[2] This is why Niccolo Machiavelli upset people so much. He strongly
pointed out that the Christian virtues, so popular at the time, were not
necessarily compatible with each other. Humility, self-sacrifice and mercy
did not fit with the virtues necessary to build a strong republic — courage, vitality, self-assertion, and dedication to the needs of the state even
if this meant overriding the needs of some individuals. (A present example would be the military draft in wartime.) That there is not one,
complete path to virtue was — and still is to many people — unsettling.

When we perceive two separate pictures of reality (as in meditation-
transcendant experience on the one hand, and ordinary sensory input on
the other), we select one as true and the other as illusion. The Hindus say
the sensory input is illusion (Maya) and the Westerner says it is truth.
Both agree that there is only one truth.

equally valid answers to problems (the Catholic error of "The Doctrine of the Double Truth"). The development of these ideas by such figures as Giambatista Vico and Friedrich Herder that different cultures have different "centers of gravity"—and arrive at different valid answers are today largely ignored. The views of Dilthey, Wildenband, and Rickert that different sciences demand different methods—that there is more than one valid path to truth—have had little effect and are very little known today in scientific circles.[3]

Since this ubiquitous idea has as its center that all genuine questions have one and only one valid answer, we think that there is one and only one correct way to *interpret reality, to behave, and to live*. Those who live in this way are living correctly, all others are living in error at best, and evil at worst. This ideal way of life is such a great and valuable goal—it implies all human beings who live it will receive the ultimate rewards, whatever the particular view considers these may be—that it is worth any sacrifice. Literally it is such a wonderful omelet that it does not matter how many eggs get broken in the attempt to reach it. War, killing, persecution, torture are all justified by the great goal to be reached. This glorious end justifies all means.

Exactly what this ideal way of being would actually be has never been widely agreed upon. We have agreed that it would be the "end of history" and, once achieved, we would dwell in

---

[3] Giambatista Vico (1688-1744) thought of many different societies. Each had "its own vision of reality, the world in which it lived, and of itself and its relation to its own past, to value and to what it strove for." Johann Gottfried Herder (1744-1803) envisioned many cultures having no sequential or other relationship to each other. Each had what he called "its own center of gravity" which differed from that of others. He believed that communities may resemble each other in many ways, but what they strive for and what they fear or worship are scarcely ever similar. Wilhelm Dilthey (1833-1911), Wilhelm Wildenband (1848-1915), and Heinrich Rickert (1863-1936) all advanced the idea that different fields of science needed basically different methods to arrive at truth.

an ideal state forever. Nothing more would be needed and nothing new would happen. These ideal states which various groups
of us have striven for in the belief that it was the only right way
for all have included a classless society, that all humanity follow our particular interpretation of the scripture we choose,
Valhalla on Earth, that all sentient beings are freed from the
Wheel of Things, that philosophers rule and all are in their
proper places in a class society of cities of about 5,000 families
each, that all humans live in harmony with our conception of
nature, that we return to the Golden Age that existed before
our own, and etc. Very few philosophers (Isaiah Berlin being
the major exception[4]) have pointed out that the concept of
Utopia contains two horrors within it. First, if attained it would
mean an end to growth, to change, to new ideas. Artists and
thinkers would have to be very carefully watched and controlled—even Plato was aware of this—and it would mean
chains about the human spirit for as long as it existed.

Second, it leads to a belief that all other goals are errors or
heresy since they are keeping the human race from fulfillment
and therefore should be suppressed. If the goal is an infinite
period (as it always is) of perfection, then the tortures of the
Spanish Inquisition were justified in inflicting a finite period of
pain to reach it. Similarly, there is justification for the SS anti-
semitic programs and the Stalinist communist killing of "devia-
tionists" of all kinds.

These two factors—that a concept of Utopia inevitably
implies restriction of new ideas and justification for the forc-
ible conversion of others—leads to what Morris Raphael Cohen
wrote of as "the fatal and desolating illusion that we can ever
have or bring about a heaven on Earth—an illusion which has

---

[4] See, for example, Isaiah Berlin, *Against the Current* (New York: Penguin, 1971) and *The Crooked Timber of Humanity* (New York: Knopf,
1991). Lewis Mumford has also discussed this point in *The Transformations of Man* (New York: Harper, 1956).

been the source of much that is noble but also of that fierce fanaticism which has shut the gates of mercy on mankind."[5] In Lewis Mumford's words:

> If intelligence dictates that there is only one right response to a given situation, only one correct answer to a question, any departure, indeed, any hesitation or uncertainty, must be regarded either as a failure of the mechanism or a perversity of the agent.[6]

Isaiah Berlin wrote in this context:

> So long as only one ideal is the true goal, it will always seem to men that no means can be too difficult, no price too high, to do whatever is required to reach the ultimate goal. Such certainty is one of the great justifications of fanaticism, compulsion, persecution.[7]

The philosopher and sociologist Karl Popper, in his classic *The Open Society and Its Enemies,* has shown how any attempt to set up a Utopia must misfire and lead to authoritarianism, the destruction of dissenters ("Liquidation" was the popular term for a long time), and the eventual diversion of movement towards an entirely different goal than was originally envisioned. This book, written far before the end of the utopian attempt made in Russia in 1917 predicted in uncanny detail the collapse of the USSR, and what the outcome of such an attempt must be.[8]

Popper describes two types of effort to change and improve society. One he calls "Utopian Engineering," and the other

---

[5] Morris Raphael Cohen, *Reason and Nature* (New York: Harcourt Brace & Co., 1931), p. 449.

[6] Lewis Mumford, *The Transformations of Man* (New York: Harper, 1956), p. 156.

[7] Isaiah Berlin, *Against the Current* (New York: Penguin, 1971), p. 78.

[8] Karl R. Popper, *The Open Society and Its Enemies,* Vol. I (Princeton, NJ: Princeton University Press, 1966), p. viii.

"Piecemeal Engineering." The utopian engineer designs a blue-
print of what the ideal society should be and tries to set it up
wholesale—to sweep away the old and start the new. Thus to
start his Republic, Plato stated that all the inhabitants of a city
over the age of 10 should be forcibly exiled, leaving only those
under that age, and the educators who would become the philosopher kings. Then the Utopia could start and attain its goal
in one giant step. Similarly, consider Pol Pot in Cambodia, who
forcibly emptied all the cities in one week, or the Stalinist com-
munists who deliberately starved to death the Kulaks (successful small farmers) in one winter to make room for the new
collectivization. Sending all the aristocrats to the guillotine in
the French Revolution led quickly to the Napoleonic monar-
chy. And etc.

The piecemeal engineer, on the other hand, is aware that
perfection is, at the very least, far distant. The real task is to
take one evil at a time—evil being regarded as that which is
most destructive and painful to people—and try to lessen it.
Regarding as equal the claim of the people now living and those
who will live in the future, the piecemeal engineer tries to reduce, one at a time, those factors which weigh most heavily on
their lives and development. Since different engineers at any
one time see different evils as the most pressing, there results
a number of simultaneous pressures in the direction of making
human life more free and having more possibilities of development and growth. But there is no attempt to sacrifice one group
for the others ("This generation is manure for the next," said
the Utopian engineer Bolsheviks of 1917 and the next following years), rather one works for specific causes, to remove one
thorn at a time from the human brow.

No one, of course, can make anybody else happy. Neither a
person nor a group can do this. Both, however, can work to
reduce the factors that make another person or group unhappy.

Nor can we make another person develop or flower. We can work to reduce the factors which prevent the flowering.

The piecemeal engineer does not see any culture as a mere means of reaching toward another. He or she is not trying to reach an ideal state because there is no such thing. (In Gertrude Stein's words, "When you get there you find there is no there there.") This kind of approach simply tries to remove one bar to human freedom and development at a time.

The concept of Utopian and Piecemeal engineering is very close to the concept of German sociologist Max Weber of "the ethics of conscience," and "the ethics of responsibility." The proponents of the ethics of conscience say in effect, "My ends are so good that all means may be legitimately sacrificed for them." It leads to fanaticism. Proponents of the ethics of responsibility point out that society creates struggles, divisions, and conflict, and therefore it is necessary to constantly compromise. The potential for corruption in this approach, said Weber, is that it can lead to a not caring and to expediency.

At one time the social activist, Abbie Hoffman, was reproached for not having a positive program, only a negative one. He was asked what he was trying to accomplish, since he did not give any picture of the utopian state he wanted to achieve. "What we want," replied Hoffman, "is a generation in which whenever a member of it walks down a street he will see three things that need to be corrected and will set to work to correct one of them."[9] It was the goal of Aldous Huxley and of George Orwell to show, in their novels, that Utopia could only be obtained by the destruction of individual differences, by a suppression of change and growth—in short that it was a terrible and destructive ideal. To show:

> That conformity kills: that men can live full lives only
> in a society with an open texture, in which variety is

---

[9] Personal communication, 1980.

not merely "tolerated" but is approved and encouraged; that the richest development of human potentialities can occur only in societies in which there is a wide spectrum of opinions—the freedom for experiments in living...that subjection to a single ideology, no matter how reasonable and imaginative, robs men of freedom and vitality."[10]

The viewpoint that there is more than one valid picture of reality, more than one valid method of attaining truth, is not easy to accept. It takes us away from the great simplicity of vision we find in the belief that we live in a world where there is one meaning to the term "rational," where we could say with the poet:

> It fortifies my soul to know
> That, though I perish, Truth is so.[11]

Always we had held to this belief. There was, we were certain, one way to understand the universe as a coherent whole and, therefore, one right way to act. Behind Buddha and Christ, behind Socrates, and Confucius, and Kant, lay this deep belief. And it again and again unleashed fury against those who believed in a different world picture and a different way of acting than we did. Without it, the potato-washing monkeys did not try to convert or exterminate the non-washers. With it, those who followed The Prophet knew that those who did not bow toward Mecca five times a day were infidels, and should be treated as such until they repented their errors or died.

The belief that there is a basic right way, and even if we have not yet exactly figured it out, we are on the correct path, gives us a basic sense of security, a sense of being at home in

---

[10] Isaiah Berlin, *The Crooked Timber of Humanity*, p. 41.
[11] Arthur Hugh Clough, "With Whom is no Variableness" in *The Oxford Dictionary of Quotations* (London: Oxford University Press, 1941), p. 141.

the universe. The assumptions, beliefs, and action patterns we were raised with are background music to our lives, and we know how to move to it. We hope to improve our knowledge of the details of reality (whether by learning how to make better social structures or better machines or better techniques of dream interpretation, or better spells and magic), and to profit by that improvement, but we do believe that that one reality is *there*. When we lose this firm knowledge, we are damaged. We become what the anthropologists call "marginal men." We suffer what the psychiatrists call "catastrophic anxiety." We become rootless, anxious; we lose our foothold, our bearings, our ability to act strongly.

We can, however, learn to maintain our own picture of reality and, at the same time, respect—and learn from—that of others and become much richer thereby. And only in this way can we—as a species—hope to survive.

In the 16th century, the philosopher Giordano Bruno wrote: "If the first button of a man's coat is wrongly buttoned, all the rest will be crooked."[12] So often in a disagreement we have the first button in the wrong buttonhole and in spite of our deepest, most sincere efforts, we cannot come to a useful conclusion. The first button is the question of how many valid ways there are of correctly or validly organizing, of construing the situation. We assume there is only one (ours) and the entire coat is crooked.

The idea of one correct view of reality, and therefore only one right way of behaving, is not only very widespread, but we do not seem to learn from experience if our own view is rejected by those in authority. From being an oppressed minority, the Christians in Roman times quickly went on to oppressing other minorities. Martin Luther's views were at first widely

---

[12] Giordano Bruno, quoted in Ernst Cassirer, *The Philosophy of Enlightenment* (Princeton University Press, 1951), p. 41.

rejected. When they became accepted in several German prov-
inces, he proposed that in those areas where he now had authority, the Anabaptists (who differed with him on some details
of theology) be tried and burned as heretics.

The Western acceptance of a variety of religions being acceptable among one's neighbors grew out of the exhaustion
after the long, vicious religious wars in Europe of the era of the
17th century. We still believed that the others were wrong and
should be corrected, but the attitude developed that it cost far
too much blood, money, and trouble, and there was no end in
sight no matter how long you fought and suffered. The fact
that one of these religious wars was called "The Thirty Years
War" gives a picture of why this sense developed. From there
it was only a short step to legislating religious freedom.

If we meet other sapient races among the stars, it is inevitable that their differences from our goals and ways of attaining them will be at least as large as our differences among
ourselves. So long as we believe that there is one and only one
correct answer to all genuine questions, a correct way of getting this answer, and that it will be in harmony with all other
"truths" we have found, we will inevitably be forced to the conclusion that the other sapients are in error and that we are in
conflict. This view must inexorably lead to disaster.

CHAPTER THREE

THE NEW SCIENCE OF THE 20TH CENTURY

The fact that we can never know what reality is, is clari-
fied by the following. A guess is made as to how things
are or work. We wish to compare it with "the truth."
What does this mean? We cannot even guess. What such
a comparison means is completely unclear.

—Albert Einstein and Leopold Infeld

The greatest invention of the 17th century was that the mechanistic interpretation of reality could be used to explain all phenomena. Once Newton had shown that the positions of the
planets could be predicted if we used the same explanatory
system as we used for levers, cogwheels, and machines in general, it quickly became accepted that this was the one true view
of reality, and that everything was explicable in this way. The
few objections from such people as Descartes were swept aside,
and presently Darwin was explaining evolution mechanistically,

Marx the development of society, and Freud the processes of the human mind.

This worked reasonably well until the appearance on the scene of Max Planck and Quantum Mechanics. He made the greatest invention of the 20th century—that everything could *not* be explained by the mechanistic view. Electrons, for example, do not behave, or even exist, in the same way machines do. They have no shape, surface, or color, and their very location is (as Werner Heisenberg pointed out) "smeared all over a probability distribution."[1] (It is not that their shape or color, etc., is unknown. They simply do not have any.) They cannot exist, or be conceived of, as standing still since their velocity is one of the numbers defining them and this cannot be zero. Planck pointed out that we do not live in "a one-tracked universe," but in a multi-tracked one. This insight was further developed by William James, Henri Poincaré, and others. At present science knows of at least five tracks; that is, five systems of explanation that are needed to deal with different realms of experience—with the phenomena we observe as we look around us and at ourselves.[2] Doubtless we will discover others, and if we meet other sapient races they will probably use still more.

The essence of the new view is that there is no one correct way to interpret reality, but only a number of convenient ones. Different realms of experience must necessarily have different systems of explanation. In one, God plays dice with the universe; in another, He does not. And both statements are equally true. In one realm of experience the Second Law of Thermodynamics is inexorable, in others it does not even exist. In one

---

[1] Werner Heisenberg, *Physics and Philosophy* (New York: Harper & Row, 1958), p. 107.

[2] These five tracks are discussed in detail in L. LeShan and Henry Margenau, *Einstein's Space and Van Gogh's Sky* (New York: Macmillan, 1982).

realm everything is quantifiable, in another this is not true. (For example, half of a book is a reasonable concept; half of an idea of a book is not.)

With Planck, science finally caught up with Nietsche's description of the idea that our senses reveal things as they "really are." He called it "The Fallacy of the Immaculate Perception." The physicist Sir Arthur Eddington wrote:

> In my observatory there is a telescope which condenses the light of a star on a film of sodium in a photo-electric cell. I rely on the classical theory to conduct the light through the lenses and focus it on the cell: then I switch on to the quantum theory to make the light fetch out electrons from the sodium film to be collected in an electrometer. If I happen to transpose the two theories, the quantum theory convinces me that the light will never get concentrated in the cell, and the classical theory shows that it is powerless to extract the electrons if it does get in. I have no logical reason for not using the theories this way round, only experience teaches me that I must not. Sir William Bragg was correct when he said that we use the Classical Theory on Mondays, Wednesdays and Fridays, and the Quantum Theory on Tuesdays, Thursdays and Saturdays.[3]

We have realized today that our very perceptions, so clear to us, and so obviously revealing "the truth," are not the only valid way of organizing the relationship between ourselves and whatever is "out there." We have learned from our families and our culture what is good and what is evil, what is beautiful and what is ugly. We have even learned what things look and sound like. Tell me what sound a rooster makes when it greets the

---

[3] Arthur Eddington, quoted in G. N. M. Tyrrell, *Grades of Significance* (London: Rider & Co., 1930), p. 56.

morning sun, and I will be able to make a pretty good guess as
to what country you spent your childhood in. If you say "Cock-
a-doodle-do," I will guess the United States. If you say
"Cocorico," I will guess France; if "Kikerikee," Germany; if
"Kikerju", Latvia; if "Cucurigoo," Romania; if "Kokke Kokkō,"
Japan; if "Kukeriko," Israel. Ask a Frenchman what is the sound
of raindrops on a window pane, he will say, "Plouf, plouf." Ask
a Japanese and he will reply, "Zaa, zaa." Ask the Frenchman
what sound a contented cat makes, and he will tell you, "Ron,
ron." Cross the border to Germany, ask the same question, and
the answer will be, "Schnurr, schnurr." When the cat is asking
for its dinner, an American will hear it say, "miaoww," a Japanese will hear "niago." Further, a Japanese mother would be
very surprised if her child's first words were "Ma Ma." She knows
a child's first words are "Ogya, ogya."

Take your dog around the world and ask what sound it
makes when it barks. The answers will vary with the country.
In France it will be "Gnaf, gnaf," in Spain, "Guau, guau," in Japan, "Wung, wung." Which of these answers is correct? None
and all. Isn't there a "true," a "right" sound that the dog makes?
How would you find out what it is? Shall we get a judge from
Africa? He will tell us that the dog goes "Kpei, kpei." Shall we
ask a computer to judge? Fine, but the answer we will get will
be determined by who programmed the computer.[4]

It is not only what we perceive, it is also how we are as
human beings that differs from culture to culture. The old idea
that there is one human nature, basically unchanging, that so
permeates our philosophy must be given up. Even the emo-
tions which we experience vary greatly from one culture to
another. What is common and accepted as natural to members

---

[4] The last three paragraphs are a paraphrase from R. Abel, *Man is the
Measure* (New York: Free Press, 1976), p. 215 ff.

of one society is viewed as weird, inexplicable, unnatural or pathological to the members of another.

The emotional state of *iklas* is well known and accepted as normal in Java. It is a static state for detachment with no conscious effect. It is the normal state for mourners at a funeral. All people raised in Czechoslovakia understand well the emotional state known as *litost*. This is a state of very strong torment caused by sudden insight into one's miserable being. It is a special kind of self-pity that can also be triggered by humiliation. The Russian *zalust* is something between pity and love, a strong positive feeling towards the helpless and lost. The belief is that only "good" people feel it. Alexander Blok has a well-known poem about a girl who is singing in the church choir and is overcome with *zalust* for all the tired in foreign countries, all those on ships at sea, and all people who have lost their joy. In the medieval period *superbia* "bad pride" was known as the "king of the vices." There is no modern English equivalent. The Latin *pietas* was a combination of loyalty, duty and affection expressed toward family, country and the gods. The Greek *apatheia* was a freedom from emotional disturbance and investment—an austere acceptance of whatever is.[5]

If we cannot even agree on what sound a dog makes when it barks, or a rooster when it crows, we certainly cannot appeal to "common sense" when it comes to moral judgments. The philosopher David Hume used the criteria of "the approval of an impartial stranger" to enable us to decide if a particular course of action is ethical. Our modern knowledge of the effect

---

[5] The previous paragraphs on different emotional states in different cultures are a paraphrase and extension of some comments of Anna Wierzbicka in her *Semantics, Culture and Cognition* (Oxford: Oxford University Press, 1992) pp. 66ff. Wierzbicka also (p. 26) gives a list of some "culture specific" terms. These words exist in some cultures and not in others. They include "mind," "anger," "fear," "depression," "freedom," "justice," "fate," and "soul."

of culture on our viewpoint as to what is right and wrong, and that there is such a diversity of cultures, makes this nonsense. Where shall we find our impartial stranger, Shall he or she be an Esquimaux who will approve of our putting aged parents out to die when they are no longer economically useful? Shall the stranger be a Fundamentalist minister from the southern United States or a Flower Child? We cannot all agree on what is, in itself, a moral act unless we choose—as we must—the essential views of our cultures, our social class and our generation. We can stand by these and, indeed, are lost unless we do to a large degree, but can find no underpinning for them in the cosmos. Unless we take our own variation of the concept of the 19th-century British middle class that "God is an Englishman," we cannot use the Hume criteria of an impartial stranger. Then we take the impartial stranger from our own group and he or she tells us our opinion is the correct one:

> From a traditional Hindu point of view everything that keeps people to the way of life that belongs to their caste is good, and what might lead them to break away is harmful. From the Marxist angle, all that makes for revolution is good and what tends to postpone it is harmful. From a Freudian position, both these kinds of harm are somewhat remote and unreal: what is really harmful is lack of self-knowledge. [6]

Montaigne put it: "One must be content to be arbitrary...since there are so many views of truth and so many experiences. One may say of life only this much, 'I will see it this way.'"[7]

---

[6] Mary Midgley, *Can't We Make Moral Judgements* (New York: St. Martin's Press, 1991), p. 68.

[7] Montaigne, quoted in H. Bevington, *Beautiful and Lofty People* (New York: Harcourt Brace, 1946), p. 11.

> We have so many different businesses with nature....
> The philosophic attempt to define nature so that no
> one's business is left out, so that no one lies outside
> the door saying "Where do I come in?" is sure in ad-
> vance to fail. The most a philosophy can hope for is not
> to lock out any interest forever." [8]

However, in taking a viewpoint that there is more than one
truth, we must be very careful not to carry it to the absurd
conclusion that there is no such thing as a truth. Writers like
Nietzsche and Michel Foucault have done this and stated that
any truth is illusion. "Truth," wrote Nietzsche, "is a mobile army
of metaphors." This is, if carried too far, nonsense. There is a
disease, known in this country as scurvy, which kills people.
Eating oranges will cure it. This is true in all cultures. It is as
true if your metaphor speaks of Vitamin C, the balance and
imbalance of humors, or of the spirits of the fruit overcoming
the demons of disease. "The fire burns the same here and in
Persia," wrote Aristotle, "but what is thought in these two places
is very different." In the words that older and more experienced professors of this and that have frequently said to their
younger, zealous, and enthusiastic colleagues, "Reality does so
exist." (Or, as Freud once put it, "Sometimes a cigar is only a
cigar.") The reality we are concerned with here is the continued existence of the human race.

---

[8] W. James, quoted in Wayne Viney, "The Cyclops and the Twelve-Eyed
Toad," in *American Psychologist*, Vol. 44, No. 10, Oct. 1989, pp. 1261-
1265. William James defined philosophical study as "the habit of always
seeing an alternative." Whenever, he said, a scientific theory becomes
"definitive" it cuts off other vantage points and hence becomes
"perspectiveless and short." A fuller description of James' insistence on
this (from which these quotations are taken) is presented by David E.
Leary in his "William James and the Art of Human Understanding," *American Psychologist*, Feb. 1992, pp. 153-160.

It is important to be aware that our traditions and behavior do not only seem "right" in themselves, they are also part of a larger picture of reality—of how-the-world-works. For example, three different individuals have the same repetitive dream. A deceased grandfather forces them to eat large quantities of a revolting dish. One says, "I had better stop eating heavy food in the evening." Another says, "I think I will call my psychoanalyst." The third says, "I wonder what my grandfather is trying to tell me." Each of these three people clearly has a different picture of reality and lives in a different world. In the first world one should stay healthy by listening to messages from the body. In the second there is such a thing as the unconscious and it is possible to get communications from it. In the third, one ought to stay in touch with ancestors. Each of these individuals has an organized and coherent world picture, an intelligible and workable metaphysical system, although he or she may not have elaborated it into a psychophysiological theory of digestion, a psychoanalytical theory of dreams, or a cosmology in which the living and the dead are equally real and existent and continue to interact.[9] If you are certain that one of these viewpoints is correct and the others are wrong, it is almost certain that the one you prefer reflects, as Suzanne Langer put it, "The metaphysics of your generation."[10]

Science, as Claude Levi-Strauss has somewhere pointed out, does not consist of reducing the complex to the simple. It consists rather of substituting a more intelligible complexity for a less intelligible one.

But intelligible to whom? This depends on your picture of reality. The Medieval theory of an imbalance of humors playing

---

[9] This is a paraphrase from Peter Berger and H. Kellner, *The Homeless Mind* (New York: Vintage-Random House, 1973), p. 13.

[10] Susanne Langer, "On Cassirer's Theory of Language and Myth," in B.A. Schlipp, ed., *The Philosophy of Ernst Cassirer* (Evanston, IL: Library of Living Philosophers, 1949), p. 381.

a part in disease rested on one picture of how the world works and what a human being is. The present-day concept of the immune system playing the same part in disease rests on another. Karma, kundalini forces, astrological influences, and chakras are part of a perfectly intelligible complexity to many people today. They are part of a completely unintelligible complexity to me.

Different complex views of reality often lead to very different conclusions as to how to act. A father and son are today discussing what the son should do now that he has finished high school. In the father's reality, the son should go on to college, work hard, learn a skill or profession, find a useful place in the culture he lives in, get married, amass enough worldly goods so that he can live comfortably and safely, and make a contribution to society in a way that will be both useful to others and help maintain the society that supports him. In the father's world view, happiness and the full life come from living in this way. In the son's reality, he should take time to find out who he really is—what likes, dislikes, aptitudes, and style most truly reflect his own personality—and seek a life that most gardens and grows his own unique being. In this view safety, happiness, and the best life comes from internal harmony, and from harmony between his natural style and his behavior, rather than from outside factors such as safe and approved work, insurance policies, and the like. If you come to the conclusion that one of these two views is more correct than the other, you are stating that one is closer to your reality than the other.

The Greek historian Herodotas reported that the King of Persia asked some Greeks what amount of money they would demand to eat the bodies of their dead fathers. They were horrified and said that nothing could persuade them to do that. The King then asked some members of a tribe that ate their dead what would persuade them to burn them as did the Greeks.

They were also horrified at the idea presented to them, and said that they would refuse to do this under any circumstances.

The Persians, of course, could be detached about the experiment. They knew that the correct way to honor the dead was to place them on high platforms and let the vultures eat them. They did not know how much this would horrify a typical 19th- or 20th-century Western European who knew that the only right way to honor the dead was to bury them in the ground and let the worms eat them.

One of the great lessons of Western philosophy has been— "Let him who is without sin cast the first stone." Whoever does not have his convictions and customs based on absolutely arbitrary choices may criticize the choices of others who do. If you eat, or burn, or expose, or bury your dead, you are making an arbitrary choice and an appeal to the gods is only answered from within you. (As Spinoza once commented, however, many people, when they think something, believe that God has told it to them.) The conventional wisdom of the time is generally taken for a law of nature.

However, the horrified reactions reported by Herodotus were not just mindless prejudice. Respect for and affection for one's own customs is both normal and essential. We must have a base for our lives—a way of organizing the world and of being in it. Without these we are empty and rootless—straws in the wind. We can and must learn to respect other customs and beliefs, and often learn new ways of being for ourselves, and new ways to act and enjoy and fulfill our existence, but without a strong preference for, and grounding in, our own, we are in quicksand. We can learn to enjoy and appreciate wine from many places, but unless the wine of home is still sweet in our mouths, we have lost our base. We cannot become complete and flourish by cutting off our roots. Joseph Conrad wrote in *Lord Jim* "A man is born into a dream as a man falls into the sea. If he tries to climb out into the air, as inexperienced people do, he drowns." [11]

Much study in our present period has been devoted to the way our language affects, and in part determines, what we can perceive and how we organize our perceptions. It is interesting to speculate how different the world must have looked before Shakespeare coined the words "assassination," "disgraceful," or "lonely"; before Thomas Gray coined the word "picturesque" in 1740, or before William Whewell coined "scientist," and "physicist" in 1837.

The basic viewpoint of this book is what various philosophers have called "conventualism," the idea that all concepts are conventions. From the viewpoint of Henri Poincaré, the mathematician and philosopher who was one of the mainsprings of this approach, even such concepts as "force," "gravity," "absolute time," and specific geometries or mechanics are conventions.

> ...the word reality maintains itself as a term of praise rather than of description....It is an expression which carries an agreeable afflatus without dependence on any particular meaning.[12]

"Experience," wrote Poincaré, "tells us not which ·is the truest geometry, but which is the most convenient."[13] Others

---

[11] Joseph Conrad, quoted in Lawrence LeShan and Henry Margenau, *Einstein's Space and Van Gogh's Sky* (New York: Macmillan, 1982), p. 20.

[12] Morris Raphael Cohen, *Reason and Nature* (New York: Harcourt Brace & Co., 1931), p. 455.

[13] Henri Poincaré, quoted in Henry Margenau, *Open Vistas: Philosophical Perspectives of Modern Science* (New Haven, CT: Yale University Press, 1961), p. 73.

who have contributed to this viewpoint include Giambatista
Vico, Johann Gottfried Herder, Ernst Mach, Max Planck, Hans
Vaihinger, Karl Pearson, William James, and Henry Margenau.
"Conventualism" is different from many modern and ancient
philosophical approaches. In these (Logical Positivism is the
extreme) any statement is meaningful only if it can be verified
in relation to my existence or my world picture. If it does not
exist or relate to my experience or world picture, it is not real,
it is not meaningful.

However, from the viewpoint of this book, there are other
equally valid experiences and other world pictures. Unless one
of these others contains an imperative—directly or indirectly—
for our destruction, we can find areas of agreement on behavior and policy. If, for example, the "Great Time" of the Australian
Aborigine is a major part of your world picture, and does not
exist in mine, we can, in spite of the very different life experiences this leads to, still agree to let each other alone, to trade
honestly, perhaps to have some of our children raised half in
your culture and half in mine, so that perhaps they might grow
up and bridge the gap, to succor each other in time of need,
etc. It only requires the respect engendered by the belief that
your world picture is as real as mine. My preference for mine
may be and should be strong, but I recognize that you walk
through existence to a different music than I do. Rudyard
Kipling wrote:

> There are nine and sixty ways
> Of constructing tribal lays,
> And-every-single-one-of-them-is-right.[14]

---

[14] Rudyard Kipling, "In the Neolithic Age," in *Rudyard Kipling's Verse*
(New York: Doubleday, 1945), p. 342.

The hardest thing for us to accept is that our model of reality is not the truth, but only a model—and at that, only one of a very large possible number of models; in short, that our deeply believed picture of the way that reality and the world are is negotiable and changeable.

Even when we are faced with the fact that we have a large number of assumptions about the nature of how-the-world-works, we rarely question these emotionally. I remember when Alfred Korzybski was giving his ten-day seminars on General Semantics in Lakeville, Connecticut in the late 1940s. One seminar was given on the third floor of the building. Korzybski opened the seminar by asking if we were comfortable. We all assured him that we were. He then asked "On what are you sitting?" After the generally humorous replies, he said, "Oh no. You are sitting on an assumption. You are forty feet above the ground and are comfortable because you all have an assumption that buildings are stable and that their floors do not collapse under you." We all knew that this was true when we heard it, but none of us felt less comfortable.

CHAPTER FOUR

THE
NEW ETHIC

Experience is a process so no point of view can ever
be the last one. Every one is insufficient and off its
balance.

—William James

The science of the 20th century has come to the conclusion
that there is no correct way to interpret reality (and therefore
to solve difficult problems), but only a most useful way. A problem is solved in terms of a particular picture of reality, its implied method of solving problems, and its implications as to
what an "answer" consists of, i.e., what type of solution it implies. We now search for useful-at-this-moment ways to construe, to organize reality. This leads directly to the new ethical
mandate. When faced with conflicting interpretations of a
situation, one keeps clearly in mind that there is always another valid way of interpreting what is going on and deciding
on a course of action.

"I do not have the only truth about this," is the operating
instruction of this guideline. An illustration would be the
symbol used by many members of the Universalist religion in
past years.

The circle illustrated the ways to truth. The small cross illustrated the Universalist way. It was off center to show it might
not be the right way or the best way for a specific person or
group. It is hard to imagine members of the Universalist group,
raised on this symbol and trained in its meaning, persecuting
the members of any other religion for their different beliefs.

Although certain self and species-protective limitations
must be woven into the guideline, it has immense power to
defuse disagreements and turn them into a mutual search for
the best answer, rather than a conflict between two different
answers. The disagreement changes from a battle of wills and
"correct" views to a scientific conference on goals and methodology with its quiet recourse to available data, new experi-
mentation, and so forth.

The United States National Forests have as their slogan
"Land of Many Uses." This has led to bitter conflicts between
environmentalists who want a "Forever Wild" protection, log-
ging companies who wish to organize the land for tree farms,
mining and oil companies, ranchers who wish to use it to graze
herds, etc. Each has seen its own view as the correct and only
correct one. The conflict has been resolved by force alone (for-
tunately so far almost completely limited to contests of strength

in political arenas). Now a new movement has arisen. This is marked by conferences over the question of the best way to use and maintain the forests in terms of present economic situations, environmental concerns, and the future needs of society. There is a gradual shifting from black and white demands, backed by whatever political clout the group can bring to bear, to a scientific search for the best way to manage the present and future situation. It is a slow but definite progress from the "I am right, my viewpoint is correct, and you are wrong," viewpoint to, "All of our viewpoints reflect a valid way of evaluating the situation and how can we get the best solution to all our viewpoints. No one viewpoint owns one monopoly on the territory of the truth."

A somewhat similar theoretical approach and the problem-solving technique to which it leads has been suggested by the philosopher Max Otto under the name of Realistic Idealism, and he points out how differerent this approach is from "compromise."

> A filling station in a small town found that it was losing customers because it was somewhat concealed from passing automobiles by big elm trees. The owners of the filling station prepared to have the elms cut down. Strong opposition arose from residents who had admired the trees for many years, and they were able to rally to their cause defenders of natural beauty in the town and the surrounding county.

> The solution...arrived at was to unite in the expense of putting up a sign at the roadside calling attention to the filling station, thus taking care of justifiable business claims, while at the same time protecting the beauty of the surroundings by saving the trees.

In compromise proceedings interest in the situation is strictly one sided. No responsibility is felt for the total eventualities and hence there is no seeking for a broader objective. The particular things desired at the beginning remain the same throughout. And what each participant ends with, and in most cases all he expected to end with, is "splitting the difference." Thereupon each intends to get more of what was originally wanted when an opportunity offers itself—giving up only what has to be given up for fear that otherwise more will be lost. There is always a novel step forward in the procedure under consideration which is lacking in compromise. And this difference is one of those vital differences which, as we say, makes all the difference in the world.[1]

Certainly all conflicts cannot be dealt with in this way, but it can prevent many power struggles. We must not expect to always (or even usually!) comprehend the other person's, group's, or non-human sapient's point of view. For example we Westerners, after much study, cannot understand the frequent Balinese trance states into which they fall as easily and quickly as we do into sleep, nor their intense devotion to local control of their affairs and not even local control by a town or a hamlet, but by literally dozens of different overlapping organizations, councils and lineage groups. We have not even been able to decide how to look at groups we classify as "savages." One anthropologist wrote:

> What, after all, are we to make of savages? Even now, after all these centuries of debate on the matter we cannot agree as to whether they are noble, bestial or

---

[1] Max Otto, *Science and the Moral Life* (New York: Mentor-NAL, 1949), p. 66.

even as you and I; whether they reason as we do, are
sunk in a demented mysticism, or are possessors of
higher forms of truth which we in our avarice have lost;
whether their customs from cannibalism to matriliny,
are mere alternatives, no better or worse than our own,
or crude precursors of our own activities, or simply
passing strange impenetrable exotica amusing to collect; whether they are bound and we are free, or we
are bound and they are free—after all this time we still
don't know. [2]

We may not understand, but we can learn to accept that there
are different valid paths and that every individual, group, or
culture has the right to go to its own heaven or hell in its own
way. That there is no "right" way to construe reality or even a
specific situation, but there is a most convenient and useful
way. Sometimes it is a particle and sometimes it is a wave, de-
pending on the analytic apparatus or concepts you are using
and what you are trying to do. This moving into, accepting as
valid, and sometimes comprehending and entering into another
construction of reality is not as esoteric or improbable as it
sounds at first. Indeed, this is what a good anthropologist does
in the field. One wrote:

What happened was not just that I very slowly began
to understand a new reality—a new culture. It wasn't
just a study and an understanding of people different
from myself, seeing their beliefs, ordering and systems
up close. I also had to go sensuously to the edge of the
world. Without having been there, felt it, smelled it,
touched it and been touched by it, I was not doing
anthropology....*What fieldwork was really all about*

---

[2] C. R. Geertz, *The Interpretation of Cultures* (New York: Basic Books,
1973), p. 345.

was being touched by a different reality. That is what
I had to "learn." It included what happened to me as
much as anything else—not just what I read and saw
and "understood" but what I ate, smelled and felt....All
of this was important, important not so much because
I began to make sense of it, ordering it, understanding
it, but because it touched me profoundly—made me
feel strong, happy, sad, frustrated, angry, tired, drunk,
bored, overwhelmed. All of those things. [3]

This approach brings to bear the single most crucial factor in
the determination of whether individuals or groups can live
together (or separated) to their greatest good. The factor is
respect. Once there is respect for other ways of construing the
situation and finding a solution, it is possible to avoid the use
of force in a very large percentage of problems. Without respect this percentage declines precipitously. John Dewey, in
his *Reconstruction in Philosophy,* wrote:

Ethical theory began among the Greeks as an attempt
to find a regulation for the conduct of life which should
have a rational basis and purpose instead of being de-
rived from culture....Ethical theory since then has been
singularly hypnotised by the notion that its business
was to discover some final end or good or some ultimate and supreme law....Some have held that the end
is loyalty or obedience to a higher power or authority;
and they have variously found the higher principle in
Divine Will, the will of the secular ruler...self-realiza-
tion, holiness, happiness, [or] in the greatest aggregate

---

[3] Kris Heggenhoughen, *The Naked Anthropologist: Tales from Around
the World,* Philip R. DeVita, ed. (New York: Wadsworth, 1991). Quoted in
N.Y. Times Book Review Section, Feb. 23, 1992, p. 35. Emphasis
Heggenhoughen.

of pleasure...the schools have agreed in the assumption
that there is a single, fixed and final good.[4]

In one way this guideline agrees with these approaches. It states
that there is, in this period of our history as never before, a
final end by means of which we can judge our conduct. Does it
protect the survival of the human race; if this is not threatened, does it protect the survival of our children; if this is also
not threatened, does it protect our own survival?

However, there is also a major way in which this approach
differs from those which Dewey describes. It is not designed to
further a particular way of behaving; not obedience to Divine
Will, doing things which are "right" in themselves, seeking the
greatest amount of pleasure, returning to the life of the good-
old-days, etc. It is designed to protect the tremendous and var-
ied potentialities and possibilities of the future, to keep our
options open by protecting racial survival. All we know about
human beings and their life in the future is that it will be *different*; that people will live in a different world than we do now
and that there are possibilities yet undreamed of. It is these—
the seeds of ways of human life contained in the mystery of the
future—which we must conserve.

The ethical mandate we are advancing here is essentially a
negative one insofar as law and legality are concerned. It does
not tell us what to do, but defines areas which must be protected. It, therefore, leaves as much as possible to individual
selection and movement. In this it follows the pattern of legal
history in the United States. In this country, if people cannot
tell the difference between right and wrong they are "not guilty
by reason of insanity." However, which of us, if we were put

---

[4] John Dewey, *Reconstruction in Philosophy*. Partially reprinted in W.
T. Jones, et al, *Approaches to Ethics* (New York: McGrawHill, 1962), p.
451. Brackets mine.

under oath, could claim that we knew and were able to explain what is right and how it differs from what is wrong? How many of us would be willing to have our sanity judged by this test?

The law solved this problem by abandoning the general question. Only the specific question,"Did he know that what he was doing was wrong?" is considered. The legal concern is only with the specific act, and with the known nature of "wrong" in this situation.

And if we look at our own personal history, most of us can recall many situations we faced in which we could not decide what course of action was right, but were certain that some specific courses were wrong.

Negative legislation is the typical instrument of a *laissez-faire* policy. Whatever is not prohibited is looked upon (we learn from our legal history) as exempt from interference. These negative statutes leave us spacious areas for individual choice. "It is rather the positive command that strips us of our choices because by prescribing one defined course, it immediately closes the way to the others." [5]

We have found that we can no longer define the "good life" in advance of knowing the individual very well. Even the most experienced psychotherapist has learned these days that he or she has no idea what the patient's problems are, or what would be a satisfactory conclusion to the therapy, until a long enough period has passed so that there is real comprehension of the world as the patient has defined it and therefore lives in. The first few sessions of a therapeutic process are like the first few pages of a novel by Dostoyevski or Tolstoi—we have had a

---

[5] Edmund Cahn, *The Moral Decision* (Bloomington, IN: Indiana University Press, 1955), p. 32. The previous four paragraphs are paraphrases of various sections of his book. Montesquieu put it: "Liberty is being allowed to do whatever the law permits." *Les Philosophes,* Norman Torrey, ed. (New York: Capricorn Books, 1960).

few glimpses of the protagonist and the protagonist's world. It is only after many chapters that we will begin to have any real sense of who the protagonist really is, and what his or her world is like. And it takes at least this long to begin to sense what would be a "good" world for him or her to live in. This cannot be defined in advance—Heaven and Hell are different for each person. For the good life to be actually good, it must be found good by the person who has to live it. There can be no judgements, for either individuals or species, as to what is the good life. Each must judge it for themselves and each of their differing judgements is equally valid.

Or, in John Stewart Mills' words: "The sole evidence it is possible to produce that anything is desirable is that people do actually desire it." [6] Spinoza put it even more clearly:

> In no case do we strive for, wish for, or desire anything because we deem it to be good, but on the other hand we deem a thing to be good because we strive for it, wish for it, or desire it. [7]

G. E. Moore, in his famous *Principia Ethica*, showed that it was impossible to define the "good" beyond this. [8]

Moral values rest on an axiom you accept as a "given," as self-sufficient in its existence, such as, "The human race should continue to exist," but it is not provable. "All men are endowed by their creator..." is not subject to proof. Nor are any of the Rights of Man, nor the Four Freedoms, nor that the strong

---

[6] John Stuart Mill quoted in W. E. Jones, et al, eds., *Approaches to Ethics* (New York: McGraw-Hill, 1962), p. 494.

[7] Spinoza, quoted in W. E. Jones, et al, eds., *Approaches to Ethics* (New York: McGraw-Hill, 1962), p. 493.

[8] G. E. Moore, *Principia Ethica* (Oxford: Oxford University Press, 1925). Thomas Hobbes wrote in *Leviathan*: "But whatever the object of any man's appetite or desire, that it is which he for his part calls good, and the object of his hate or aversion, evil."

should not enslave the weak. You cannot prove any of these. You can accept them as part of a worldview, and live by them, and fight for them, and perhaps die for them. But do not expect a proof of them, or a repeatable experiment demonstrating them.

Some of them, such as, "All men are endowed..." and that the strong should not exploit the weak, which now appear self-evident, would have sounded pretty silly to a Greek or Roman philosopher, a Medieval scholar, or just about anyone else before the 16th century. And there were a lot of centuries and a lot of cultures and a lot of very bright men and women back there.

꙳ ꙳ ꙳

"Proof" simply means "test" as in the proof of the pudding, or in Aberdeen Proving Grounds. The kind of test needed varies with the kind of thing being tested. When we are doubtful about a moral judgement, what we need is to have it more fully explained to us, and we need the reasons for and against it more clearly stated. Value judgements arise naturally from a worldview, a picture of how and what reality is and works. We can only communicate a worldview, we cannot prove it. We can evaluate the kind of life it leads to and see how we feel about it. We can contrast it to the world pictures in and by which others live. Sometimes we can comprehend that both are true, and we choose one. We can learn new truths and ideas from each other, or realize that we prefer to leave each other alone. But neither is correct except for us or for them.

In Gotthold Lessing's drama, *Nathan the Wise,* the Sultan asks Nathan which of the three religions—Judiasm, Christianity, Mohammadanism—is the true one. He says that Nathan is not the sort of person to remain "where chance of birth has cast you," but would choose the correct religion through study and insight. Nathan replies with the story of the three rings.

In a far country, says Nathan, lived a wealthy man who had a very precious ring. "The stone it held, an opal, shed a hundred colors fair, and had the magic power, that he who wore it, trusting its strength, was loved by God and man." [9]

In his family, this ring was handed down by each owner to his favorite son, who then became prince of the house. This went on for many generations until one father had three sons, all of whom he loved equally, and loved so much that he could not bear to disappoint any of them. This man, over the years, promised the ring privately to each of the three. When age came upon him and he was close to death, he secretly had a jeweler make two rings identical with the one he wore and, before he died, called each son into his room and gave him one of the rings. After his death the sons argued and bickered over which was the true ring and finally brought the matter before a judge. The judge offered first his verdict—that judging from the sons' behavior, the original ring had been lost and all three were counterfeit. Then he said that if the sons would take his counsel, not his verdict, he would point out that the effect of the true ring, as of the true religion, was inward, not outward—that is, for the person who trusted it, it helped to lead the kind of life where he would "be loved by God and man." The judge said that the father had loved the sons so much he had given them rings which could not be distinguished by their form, but only by their effect. Let each son strive to bring out the magic of the opal in his ring by living a life of love, peacefulness, doing good. If each believed in his ring and acted to bring out the best in it, then we would see in future years, by the effect it had, which

---

[9] Gotthold E. Lessing, *Nathan the Wise,* Bayard Morgan, tr. (New York: Frederic Ungar, 1955). This and the following pages refer to Act 3, Scenes 5 and 7 (first published in 1779).

was the true ring. The children and children's children of the owner would indeed "be loved by God and man."

This, said Nathan, is the only possible answer to the question of which of the three religions is the correct one. Each person born into one will tend to believe in it. This is because all religions are based on their history, and we must accept or reject history on faith. And we are least likely to doubt the history told us by our family. It is not only that they are closest and "have given us proofs of love," but it has become, by the time we grow up, a part of us. "The superstition in which we grew up, though we may recognize it, does not lose its power over us." However, the "truth" of a religion, its essence, can only be determined by observing the effect it has on the behavior of its believers.

In discussion over values:

> It is very important that the point of discussion is explanation rather than proof. If someone makes an unexpected value judgement, the last thing that reasonable bystanders might be expected to say is, "prove it." Their more natural response is likely to be "Oh, but what do you mean?" "Proof" is a term that belongs particularly to facts. [10]

It is not possible to show objective reasons why it is desirable that the human race survive. A rat, or a giraffe, or a sea otter would doubtless not see it as desirable. But we are human beings and we do desire it and it is therefore "good" for us. Only

---

[10] Mary Midgley, *Can't We Make Moral Judgements?* (New York: St. Martin's Press, 1991), p. 142.

an extremely damaged human being would not wish this outcome. Some philosophers seem to so lose their relationship
with the human condition (at least in their writing in learned
journals) that they seem to approach this extremely damaged
condition. Thus one well-known contemporary philosopher
wrote:

> It is not imperative that any individual, or any nation,
> or even the race itself should even continue to exist. It
> is imperative that so long as we live we do so with taste
> and intelligence, with finess and generosity. [11]

This is fine and inspiring prose and would go well in a Fourth
of July or a Bastille Day speech. It has nothing to do with how
we humans actually feel or are prepared to act. It is not only
that it is semantic nonsense since one person's taste is another's
repugnance, but it is also that we want our species to survive,
and it is therefore not only desirable, but in the last analysis
the closest we can come to a human moral imperative. [12]

In the 1930s, Jean Piaget started his immensely influential and
seminal studies on the personality development of children.
He demonstrated that their play was a major influence on their
moral development. Playing according to the rules of the
game—immutable until change is agreed on—leads to the
sense of justice, fairness, reciprocity (sauce for the goose), and

---

[11] Alexander Meiklejohn, quoted in Max Otto, *Science and the Moral
Life* (New York: Mentor-NAL, 1949), p. 103.

[12] "...in imaginary extinction we gaze past everything human to a dead
time that falls outside the human tenses of past, present, and future...we
find that almost everything that might engage our attention, or stir our
interest—even if only to repel us—has passed away." Jonathan Schell,
The Fate of the Earth (New York: Knopf, 1982), p. 140.

punishment for infractions. Peer relationships in the games leads to the recognition of "acting right" to maintain these relationships and the game. The sense of "Do unto others" is developed here. Certainly there are also hierarchical relationships in the in-group. The person who is "it" behaves quite differently than the others. In fact, children's play leads to the rules for the in-group—the rules necessary for the in-group to be maintained.

The philosopher Ernst Cassirer was once asked why he did not write a book on ethics. He replied that there was no point to this idea, that ethics were "self-evident." [13] For a man of such tremendous capacity and learning as Cassirer to make such a statement is startling and raises a question. In view of all the work done by philosophers in this field, what in the world did he mean by it?

We are led by this question to one of the major problems in ethics. The Western philosophers, often starting from very different points, and with very different assumptions and methods, all end up with pretty much the same general conclusions as to how we ought to live and what an ethical life is like. In addition they are here in basic agreement with the great Eastern philosophers, such as Confucius and Chuang Tzu. How is it that almost no matter where they started—there is a God or there is not, humans are basically good or basically evil, the universe cares or it does not, and so forth—they all tend to advise us to live our lives in pretty much the same way?

What is "self-evident" about ethics are the general rules of behavior which are necessary if a group is to survive. From an army to a cocktail party, from a family to a hunting group, there are certain rules which are necessary for it to continue to function. These are the rules that children learn in their play. Speak-

---

[13] Personal communication between Anne Cassirer Appelbaum and author, 1992.

ing generally because groups are so different, we might categorize them as follows:

1. Everyone knows how to interpret the words and gestures of others. We know which mean specifically what they say and which do not. I believe train announcers and published stock market figures. I do not believe comedians. I do not hold politicians running for election to their words although I may reproach them with the words. I move when the command is preceded by "Simon Sez" and do not move when it is not thus preceded.

2. The general rules for behavior and status are not changed without warning and at whim. People are punished for transgressing these rules. Contracts are kept and there are ways of enforcing them.

3. Reciprocity exists in certain behaviors and hierarchical relationships exist in others. It is clear which is which.

4. "Fairness" is a well-defined term and seen as important.

5. The safe times and places are known. For example, one can afford to sleep without an armed guard if this is done in the correct times and places. Violations of the safe times and places are publicly punished.

6. The in-group is carefully defined. Different rules govern the members of the out-group.

The general advice given us by ethical philosophers as to how to live our lives is essentially methods as to how to be sustained by and to sustain an in-group. Although the specific advice varies from philosopher to philosopher, the different general guidelines do not contradict each other. [14]

These necessary rules for a group to continue to function are learned in childhood play. This book is essentially a discussion

---

[14] L. Mothershead, *Ethics* (New York: Holt, Rinehart, Winston, 1955), p. 136.

of why, today, all human beings—and all other sapients we meet—must be treated as members of the in-group if our species is to survive.

A key event in the long, slowly developing history of humanity was the issuing of the papal bull *Sublimis Deus* of Pope Paul III in 1537. This stated that the American Indians and the blacks of Africa were human and had souls. This recognized that there is an intrinsic unity in the human race, that differences must be seen as relative, and that we all belong to the same family. We are different in our looks and behavior and beliefs, but we are all human.

In the future we hope for—and may desperately need—a new bull, extending this further, at the least to all sapients, all those who have intelligence, no matter how much it differs from our own.

To bring up to date a point that Hegel made in his *Lectures on the Philosophy,* we might say that in ancient civilizations, one person was free. In Graeco-Roman times, some people were free. In modern times many people are free. The more people who are free in the next period of history, the more likely we are to survive.

We are, in this book, as John Dewey urged over and over, treating moral and factual problems in the same way. There has been a strong tendency in philosophy and in everyday thought to treat them quite differently.

People tend to treat moral problems as radically different in kind from technical problems and accordingly, as calling for radically different types of solutions. Problems of means, they are quite content to resolve by means of hypotheses tested in experiment and alterable in the light of further experience. Problems of ends, they think, cannot be solved in this way. [15]

Dewey pointed out that the ends and the means can only be separated if we are talking in the abstract where they do not really exist. In the concrete, the real situation, the ends and the means form a "Gestalt," an integrated dynamic whole where all the parts influence each other. "The 'end' is merely a series of acts viewed at a remote stage; and a means is merely the series viewed at an earlier one....Means and ends are two names for the same reality." [16]

They are interacting if only on psychological grounds. The way we work toward our goals influences and defines us. The goals are therefore changed by the means. There are, said the medical philosopher and physician Graham Bennette,[17] two ways of getting to the top of a particular mountain. One way is the north face where you climb at tremendous effort, hanging on by toes and fingertips, and are at great risk. The other way is the south face where you comfortably and safely ride up on the cable car. And when you get to the top the view is exactly the same except that it is completely different.

Whatever is done affects the outcome. Our experience is continuous.

---

[15] John Dewey, *Human Nature and Conduct* (New York: Modern Library, 1930), pp. 34 ff.

[16] John Dewey, *Human Nature and Conduct*, pp. 34 ff.

[17] From personal communication between author and Graham Bennette, M. D., Secretary of British Cancer Council, London, 1988.

It is tempting and easy to talk about ends and means in the abstract and not to be clear about how different this is from the concrete situation. In a way this is a perfect example of the validity of Wittgenstein's statement that, "philosophy is a struggle against the bedevilment of language."

Further, in the present situation, Machiavelli's concept of private and public morality being separate and different does not hold true. If our goal is racial survival, then the two become one.

A. We will be judged on both by alien races if we meet any.
B. We will judge ourselves, and our children will judge us similarly on both. This judgment by our children will strongly affect their behavior in ways which may well determine our survival. We cannot teach them one kind of morality if we practice another.

In the 1920s there were two leading schools of philosophy in Europe; that led by Martin Heidegger and those who followed Ernst Cassirer. A debate between the two was organized in 1928 in the city of Davos, in Switzerland. It was set up as if it were a championship heavyweight boxing match. Philosophers from all over Europe attended and lined up behind their champion. Heidegger was known as a combative and argumentative personality, with little respect for anyone else's point of view. Although Cassirer had a quite opposite reputation, everyone expected a fierce and fiery debate. No one expected their viewpoint to be changed or the division between the two schools to be made any less, but all expected to enjoy the brilliant pyrotechnics and the discomfiture of their opponents.

At the beginning of the discussion, Cassirer said "I do not understand what you mean by the concept of 'anxiety.' I do not know what it is. Can you help me be clear about it? [18] Heidegger smiled, relaxed, and the two leading philosophers of Europe disappointed everyone there by implicitly agreeing that rather than fighting they should look together for common assumptions and common goals, and that there might be two—at least—different legitimate paths to understanding the human condition. The great debate never came off. Instead there was a long and fruitful discussion of where each of them came from, where they were trying to go, and on how much they agreed.

Although after this there were still major differences between the two schools, they were no longer seen as antagonistic. Philosophers from both could teach in the same department peacefully and cooperatively.

---

[18] Ernst Cassirer, from personal communication with Anne Cassirer Applebaum, 1994. The event was widely reported and discussed at the time.

CHAPTER FIVE

WHAT IS CONSIDERED TO BE REAL?

If you try to explain to someone, say in the steel industry, that possibly prosperity in other countries might be advantageous to him, you will find it quite impossible to get him to see the argument, because the only foreigners of whom he is vividly aware are his competitors in the steel industry. Other foreigners are shadowy figures in whom he has no emotional interest.

—Bertrand Russell

I have never been to Sardinia. I know intellectually that such an island exists. I am sure that there are people living there. I dimly remember looking at the pictures of a *National Geographic* article on it. But it is far less real to me than is Long Island, where I have been many times, and on which are placed most of the memories of my childhood. Further, I have many friends who live there, and I often telephone or see them. Several times a year I still go there on one errand or another.

Although I intellectually know that both of these places exist, one is far more real to me than the other. As I look at this, it seems clear to me that all my experiences and memories can be classified in this way—as more or less real to me. It is as if I am subjectively surrounded by a vast field divided by concentric circles with no sharp demarcations. The circles make zones of reality around me. Closest to the center are the things most real to me—here is my own existence, my body, my clothes, my loved ones, my home and so forth. Gradually the reality is leached out of things as I progress further and further away from the center. Further toward the periphery are Williamsburg, Virginia (where I went to school) over nearly 50 years ago and about which I think from time to time, my army induction at Fort Crook, Nebraska in World War II, and the stamp collecting I did as a child which I am often briefly reminded of when a foreign letter arrives, or when I see a new commemorative stamp in the post office. Further yet toward the periphery are Sardinia, North Dakota where I have never been, United States President Chester A. Arthur (1884-1888), the other side of the Moon, and the novels of Walter Pater which I have never read.

The place of things in these zones, how real they are to me, appears to be determined by three factors: how much I am in contact with them; how much I interact with them; how much I have them on my mind.

As I am a professional psychologist, Freud is more real to me than John Maynard Keynes, mental health is more real than treasury notes. Our personal history and professional malformations makes some things likely to be more real than others. Compare the contents of the reality zones of a New York stockbroker, a Basque sheepherder, a Chinese Communist Party official, a California surfer, and a British major of the Royal Marines. The sociologist Max Weber once said that people are animals suspended in webs of significance that they themselves have spun. The classical definition of "culture" is that it consists of whatever we have to know or believe in order to operate in a manner acceptable to its members. How very different this is in the culture of any of the above individuals. And these are only a very few of the cultures we know.

There can never be a quantitative description of how real things are to me.[1] And many human areas are dealt with much better when we do not make exact definitions. "It is the mark of an educated mind," wrote Aristotle, "not to put more precision into an area than the area contains." There are, however, certain general remarks I can make about the reality of things to an individual. For example, by all three criteria, I am always the most real thing to me. (The lover changes this when he insists, against all the evidence of his senses, that he and his beloved are one.) Second, I will make priority decisions on the basis of which things seem more real and which less real. Thus, if I am a politician, the chances are that I read books which I buy or get in the mail whether sent to me or ordered after I read the reviews. In all probability I will not use the Public Library very much. I will not have much contact with the Public Library, will not interact with it very much; will not have it very much on my mind. Therefore, whatever my overall intellectual belief systems or campaign promises, if a budget crunch comes, I will tend to cut library funds. Since (today) I am very much in contact with, and interact with, computers, I will consider them as more real and therefore higher on my priority list. Budget crunch or no, I will probably find the money to buy computers for government or schools. As another example, I

---

[1] The reason that there can never be a quantitative description of human feelings or perceptions is detailed in my book, *The Dilemma of Psychology: A Psychologist Looks at His Troubled Profession* (New York: Dutton, 1991).

will probably be in a private car far more than in buses or trains. Therefore, it is far more likely I will find money for roads and highways more easily than for these forms of public transportation. This is also demonstrated in the difference between the government subsidies given to airplane companies as compared to those given to bus systems. Politicians travel frequently by air—airplanes are real to them.

In the time this book is being written, we, in the United States, have a growing problem with which we seem unable to deal. This is the fact that increasingly large numbers of people do not have homes to live in and cannot afford to rent or buy one. This is surely not a problem beyond our intellectual and economic resources—we need only recall how we mobilized the entire nation to a war footing in 1942 and in a matter of months built hundreds of army camps and supplied them with everything necessary for soldiers to live in them. Where it was needed, civilian housing sprang as quickly into existence. The techniques, knowhow, and physical resources needed for the present task are far less than were needed for that one. However, the problem keeps growing and we do very little or nothing.

This is not due to ill will to our fellow man or to "laziness" or anything of that sort. It is rather that those who have the power to set up programs and implement them live in homes and are, unless they happen to meet a homeless person in the street, shielded from the problem. It is simply not in the inner zones of the real for them. The only ones for whom the problem is truly real are the homeless themselves and the few with homes who work with them, are involved in and constantly thinking about the fact that there are more and more people with no place to live. Unless this is taken into account, our do-nothing behavior in the face of this increasing disaster is simply not comprehensible.

Since *I* am always the most real thing to me and *now* the most real time, there is a very real tendency to make decisions in terms of what I perceive as immediate or short-term gains rather than in terms of less real future possibilities. The implications of this for such problems as the ecological disaster that we are heading toward and the population problem are clear. I am more in contact with present factors than future ones, I interact with them more, I have them more on my mind. Therefore (as in the "library" example), I will tend to make decisions more in terms of present factors than future ones. Thus the difficulty people have in dieting when the food in front of them is much more real than the hypothetical weight loss in the future. The future is generally less real than the present. When it is an undated and unspecified future, it becomes even less real. Once this concept is clearly understood it will be possible to deal more effectively with education, ecological, and population matters.

The task in dealing with disputes between people or with other sapients is first to be aware that there are valid differences among the disputants as to what is most real. Second is to be interested in, respect, and try to find out what these differences are. When we do not do this, their behavior is not comprehensible to us and we tend to categorize them as irrational, unreasonable, primitive, barbaric, schizophrenic, or some other variant of the "other morés, other beasts" point of view.

A lack of understanding of this concept often leads us to surprise and consternation when an argument, logical and conclusive, fails to produce the results we expect. We believe that if we can make someone understand something then it will be as real to him or her as it is to us; that he or she will be affected by it as much as we are. This is simply not true. To give a rather extreme example, the ancient Greeks well understood the concept of robots and mechanical servants. In *The Illiad*—with which all educated Greeks were familiar, and whose stories most of the rest had heard from time to time—are clear descriptions of mechanical, self-moving serving tables for banquets (373-377) and of the construction of robot women (417-420). In another well-known tale of the period (*The Argonauts*) is a clear description of a robot tank. However, these concepts were just not in the inner zones of the real—and so there was very little interest in them. To understand and to consider real (and therefore to act in terms of) are two very different things.

Although the idea of atoms had been known since Democritis in the classical Greek times, the general Western population only accepted them as "really real" after Hiroshima and Nagasaki. It is not only our knowledge of specific concepts such as robots and atoms—which become more or less real over time. It is also our more general beliefs about what is right and important and good. These also vary not only between societies, but also in the same society at different times. In an example given by Isaiah Berlin:

> ...many of the most familiar values of our own culture are more recent than what might at first be supposed. Integrity and sincerity were not among the attributes which were admired—indeed they were scarcely mentioned—in the ancient or medieval worlds, which prized objective truth, getting things right, however accomplished. The view that variety is desirable whereas uniformity is monotonous, dreary, dull, a fetter upon the free-ranging human spirit...stands in sharp contrast with the traditional view that truth is one, error many, a view scarcely challenged before—at the earliest— the end of the Seventeenth Century. The notion of toleration, not as a utilitarian expedient to avoid destructive strife, but as an intrinsic value; the concepts of liberty and human rights as they are discussed

> today; the notion of genius as the defiance of rules by
> the untrammelled will...all these are elements in a great
> mutation of thought and feeling that took place in the
> Eighteenth Century. [2]

The observation that what we usually consider right or wrong
is determined by the society we grew up in is reinforced by the
knowledge that the term "ethics" comes from a Greek word
meaning "customs," or "habits," and the word "morals" from a
Latin word with the same meaning.

When we constantly interact with something, when we think
about it extensively, when it is very much on our minds, it becomes most real to us and very often becomes ethically valid
and ethically positive for its own sake. We lose all other judgements of it and see it as right because we are doing it. Many
atomic scientists in the early 1940s joined the Manhattan Project
with many misgivings, but felt that the fact that the Germans
were working on a similar project gave them moral justification for trying to build such a bomb before Hitler obtained one.
In spite of the fact that it was well known to them that the
Japanese had no such project underway, on the day Germany
surrendered only one scientist resigned from the program. The
work itself had become its own ethical justification. For some
deeply involved in a field, this goes even further. A Manhattan
Project scientist writes:

---

[2] Isaiah Berlin, *Against the Current* (New York: Penguin, 1982), p. 333.
"I remember as a child having great difficulty in realizing that while the
dome of heaven had its highest point directly over where I was, others
living far off thought that the same was true for them. A similar realization in the moral realm is far more difficult." Morris Raphael Cohen, *Reason and Nature* (New York: Harcourt Brace, 1931), p. 427.

In 1946 I asked Enrico Fermi, the Nobel laureate and the physicist responsible for the first nuclear chain reaction, 'Now that you have achieved your goal, how do you feel about it?' Fermi, in his quiet, unemotional voice, answered, 'I was put on this earth to make certain discoveries. I am not interested nor concerned about what the politicians do with them.'" [3]

Liddell Hart, the military historian, writes of German general Heinz Guderian (who was largely responsible for the development of the German tank division and the "Blitzkreig"), that he had "the passion of pure craftsmanship." [4] Guderian's autobiography, written after the war and while he was living in West Germany, refers to Hitler and politics, but only as they helped or hindered his plan to improve military efficiency. He was almost completely detached from who would use the armored force he was designing or for what ends. Working on the perfection of his panzer divisions he wrote, "The year 1937 passed peacefully." A historian of modern Europe would surely disagree. During the war an army order came down from Hitler permitting "excesses against civilian populations" and barring any punishment for whatever soldiers did to civilians. Guderian did not pass this order on to his own troops "because discipline must suffer if it were published." There is no mention of any other reasons for not publishing the order.[5] This, of course, reminds one of Adolf Eichmann who could never understand what he did wrong—in his view what was important was that he "did a good job" and was efficient at it.[6]

---

[3] Mario Salvadori, "Fermi's Nuclear Policies," in *The Sciences,* March-April 1992, p. 55.

[4] Liddell Hart in Heinz Guderian, *Panzer Leader* (New York: Ballantine, 1952).

[5] Heinz Guderian, *Panzer Leader* (New York: Ballantine, 1952), p. 126.

[6] Adolf Eichman, in Hannah Avendt, *Eichmann in Jerusalem* (New York: Viking, 1963), p. 86.

Our work, being among the things that are most real to us, often leads to a sense that it is valid and right in its own existence. We might call this the "Craftsman's Imperative." Instead of a means, our work becomes an end. It can lead to strange places, such as the belief that the atom bomb should be built after Hitler's program no longer existed, the development of the panzer division and the Blitzkrieg, the high efficiency of Eichmann's system to send Jews to gas chambers, and even to what people involved in medical ethics have called the "Technological Imperative"—the medical belief that just because the technology exists, it should be used regardless of whether or not it is in the best interests of the patient.[7]

The "Craftsman's Imperative" can lead us to strange and extreme places. So often the attacks on "whistleblowers"—those who go public with the details of what is wrong with a project—are clearly motivated by far more than the desire of others working there to protect themselves. There is the belief that the whistleblower is doing something evil by endangering the project itself, and should be prevented from doing so at all costs. The murder of Karen Silkwood (while on her way to a meeting—with the USA commission regulating atomic energy plants—with information about the major problems at the atomic energy plant) and the threats later made to and attacks on others who attempted to publicly complain, are cases in point. It was not self-protection that led those ordering the killing to risk a murder charge to protect themselves from what could only have been far lesser charges; it was a belief that their work, which had become an end and not a means, was threatened. What is most real to us—such as the work into which we put so much of our heart and brain and time and caring—becomes valid and critical to continue in its own right.

---

[7] Nancy Dubler and Davin Nimmons, *Ethics on Call* (New York: Crown-Harmony, 1992), pp. 73 ff.

Since we are largely guided in our thoughts and feelings by
those things most real to us—the forces and entities we interact with most and which are most on our minds—a curious
general belief frequently tends to color our thoughts and our
planning. This is the confidence that we can get the best guid-
ance simply from consulting the direction in which we are already traveling. Thus if a company, college, or town increases
in size, this is a good thing and the growth should continue.
Similarly the speed of travel, number of highways, population
size (of a country, city, or town), the power of automobiles,
and so forth. This is perhaps more true in the 20th century
than it has been in many previous ones. During this time, for
example, art criticism has been dominated by the idea of the
Avant-garde, which means a body of troops marching ahead of
the rest of the army. But along what road we hardly ask. Moving fast and ahead implies a definite journey toward a desired
(even though perhaps unattainable) goal. In the 19th century
the art establishment identified it with the perfection of the
older modes of art—classicism. Today it identifies itself with
the avant-garde itself.

Humane and liberating policies are called "progressive,"
or, "It is the next step." Present-day inhumane laws, customs,
or conditions are called "Victorian" or "Medieval." This is not
based on the popular reverence for Darwin. His theory is about
the way species adapt to changing conditions. It says nothing
about a fixed upward course. (He only used the word "evolution" once in his writings.)

Humans certainly do not agree on what is most real or un-
real. Voltaire tells the story of the Native American who wan-
dered into a building of the Spanish Inquisition. He simply could
not understand why one group of people wanted another to
change their verbal statements about God or why the second
group refused. Different things were in different zones of real-

ity for the Indian and the Spaniards. The early Dutch on the island of Manhattan who bought something very real to them (ownership of land) from Indians to whom this concept was very far out in their zones of reality is another case in point. On a smaller scale, but illustrating the point, the educator John Esty tells the story of the first-grade daughter of a college professor friend of his. In her reading workbook was a page on the word "work." There were two pictures: one of a man chopping wood, the other of a man reading a book. She had to circle the picture showing "a man at work." Of course she got it wrong.[8]

Once this concept is accepted and used in disputes (as good labor mediators have been doing for a long time), many disputes will be defused. At the least the implied respect for the other's way of organizing reality will make it clear which disagreements can be solved without the judgement of force and which cannot.

---

[8] John C. Esty, "The Lamp of Learning, Not the Shoehorn," in Frederick Raubinger and Harold Rowe, *The Individual and Education* (New York: Macmillan, 1968), p. 309.

CHAPTER SIX

LIMITATIONS AND IMPLICATIONS OF THE NEW ETHICAL GUIDELINE: THE RULE OF THREE

We look at things not only from different sides, but with different eyes.

—Pascal

All philosophical and metaphysical systems oversimplify—none can be more than general guidelines. The world we live in cannot be adequately described in a manner less complex than it is in actual form and substance. No guidebook can describe every bump and twist of a road, but it can point out the existence of the road, its general direction, and where you are likely to arrive if you take it or if you follow another road. In the words of the philosopher Alfred North Whitehead: "The defect of a metaphysical system is that it is a neat little system of thought, which thereby oversimplifies its expression of the world."[1]

There are no definite, always true, final answers in this field. We need an orientation and general rules, but difficult questions still still have to be solved with hard study. Whomever looks in ethics for an absolute law—like Boyle's Law or the relationship of the diameter and circumference of a circle—is chasing illusion and moonbeams.

Immanuel Kant opened his discussion of ethics with the statement, "Nothing can possibly be conceived, in the world or out if it, that can be called good without qualification, except a good will." To follow any rule at all times, to "Do right even if the sky falls," not to lie or steal in certain circumstances because "It is always wrong," is the Puritan way. This leads to the man who Mark Twain called "A good man in the worst sense of the word." In the old and well-studied case, Heinz is right to steal the medicine from the pharmacy in order to save his wife's life, and which he cannot obtain in any other way.

In this ethical mandate we do not have, nor would we wish to have, a tight, organized system with an absolute turn-to-page-58-for-the-answer approach to each question. There will be far too many problems and many of them are, in principle, unpredictable. And since such concepts of justice are related to a particular concept of what a human being is, it would also be limited to a particular culture and time. What we do have here is a set of guidelines that can be applied to many problems. Many other problems will have to be solved according to the particular society, mores and customs in which they exist.[2]

---

[1] Alfred North Whitehead, *Religion in the Making* (New York: Macmillan, 1926), p. 41.

[2] "...no philosophy can ever be anything but a summary sketch, a picture of the world in abridgement, a foreshortened bird's-eye view of the perspective of events." William James, *A Pluralistic Universe* (Cambridge: Cambridge University Press, 1977), p. 9 (originally published in 1909).

There is not, and there can probably never be, an ethical guideline which gives neat and precise answers to all dilemmas of how to act. Human life is far too complex and we are involved in too many interwoven webs of relationships for there ever to be a mathematical formula which tells us how to act in the new situations which constantly arise. There is often simply no right answer to an ethical problem, but a variety of possible courses of action. Each person will have to choose the one which seems best to that person at that time. Jean-Paul Sartre, in his *Existentialism is a Humanism*, gives a typical example, describing:

> ...one of my students who came to see me under the following circumstances: his father was on bad terms with his mother and, moreover, was inclined to be a collaborationist; his older brother had been killed in the German offensive of 1940, and the young man, with somewhat immature but generous feelings, wanted to avenge him. His mother lived alone with him, very much upset by the half-treason of her husband and the death of her older son; the boy was her only consolation.

> The boy was faced with the choice of leaving for England and joining the Free French Forces—that is, leaving his mother behind—or remaining with his mother and helping her to carry on. He was fully aware that the woman lived only for him and that his going off— and perhaps his death—would plunge her into despair. He was also aware that every act he did for his mother's sake was a sure thing, in the sense that it was helping her to carry on, whereas every act he made toward going off and fighting was an uncertain move which might run aground and prove completely useless; for example on his way to England he might, while passing

through Spain, be detained indefinitely in a Spanish camp; he might reach England or Algiers and be stuck in an office at a desk job. As a result, he was faced with two very different kinds of actions; one concrete, immediate, but concerning only one individual; the other concerned an incomparably vaster group, a national collectivity, but for that very reason was dubious and might be interrupted en route.[3]

And, indeed, it is important that we do not search or even hope for absolutes. In philosophy, these are sublime structures, but when applied rigidly, they destroy the individual and damage those around him. They never quite fit the specific case.

...the moral ideal is a compass point, not a destination; while a fixed orientation to north and south is essential in order to find one's way to port, one may have to tack one's ship, now to the east, now to the west, in order to move in the general direction one has chosen; while if one sets one's course unconditionally to north or south, one will find oneself at last only in a polar waste. One steers by the fixed North Star, not in order to reach an ideal north, but in order to find a fair haven.[4]

Only at Greenwich observatory, itself, does ideal and absolute time exist. When we leave the immediate area of Greenwich we find that our clocks must be adjusted to local time, lest we sleep in the daytime and call on our neighbors when they are in bed. We need the absolute and ideal time of Greenwich, but

---

[3] Jean-Paul Sartre, *Existentialism is a Humanism,* partially reprinted in W. Jones, *Approaches to Ethics* (New York: McGrawHill, 1962), p. 523.

[4] Lewis Mumford, *The Conduct of Life* (New York: Harcourt Brace, 1951), p. 116.

to live only by it and not to take account of local conditions and latitude brings only disaster and damage. "Indeed, the more stubbornly one adheres to a system, the more violence one does to life."[5] Even the armor of self-righteousness we feel when we abide by the strict letter of the law will not save us.

The search for truth must never be confused with the human need for certainties. Truth is ever growing and developing. Certainty is stable forever you hope and believe. You confuse the two at your peril.[6] The Earl of Balfour wrote in 1905:

> Our highest truths are but half truths,
> Think not to settle down forever in any truth.
> Make use of it as a tent in which to pass a summer night
> But build no house of it or it will be your tomb.[7]

In spite of our basic feeling that there is somewhere a way of attaining a final basic harmony in which all our ideals will fit together, this idea is not attainable. Is it freedom we seek as the end? Total freedom for the wolf means death for the lamb. Should we resist tyranny even at the risk of the lives of our children and our parents? How much should the artist sacrifice others for the sake of his or her ideal? How much liberty should we curtail in order to insure that the hungry are fed, the rain forests protected, the oceans unsullied? How do we— or do we—protect the weak from the strong without taking away the liberty of the strong? The Talmud states that it is not permissible to tell a lie except to the very ill. What do we do when a murderer asks if his proposed victim, who is hiding in

---

[5] Richard Hofstadter, *Social Darwinism in American Thought* (New York: George Braziller, 1969), p. 176.

[6] Richard Hofstadter, *Social Darwinism in American Thought*, p. 130.

[7] Earl of Balfour, quoted in G. N. M. Tyrrell, *Grades of Significance* (London: Rider & Co., 1930), p. 79.

your house, is within? Freedom and liberty are essential for the best hope of our species survival, but how much?[8] George Bernard Shaw wrote in the Preface to *Getting Married*, "There is no more dangerous mistake than the mistake of supposing that we cannot have too much of a good thing."[9]

Further, we have learned to our sorrow that no solution leads to an end of problems. Each creates its own. The safety of walls in the Medieval period led to plague. Free and open science led to atomic waste; free enterprise to monopolistic practices and to environmental disasters. Absolute justice clashes with mercy.

All principles must be kept from extremes if we are to be able to live with them. In the ancient tale from the Zohar (a Medieval mystical manuscript), God first made the world of Justice. It was too brittle and soon broke. He then made it of Mercy. It was too soft and could not cohere. He then made it of equal parts of Justice and Mercy and it held together.

If we wish to keep open the options of the human race and not try to force the conventional wisdom on which we were raised on everyone, we must be aware of how widespread and deep is the belief that there is a correct way. There is, in the United States, an old leftist saying: "Inside every liberal is a fascist struggling to get out and run things the correct way in the name of democracy, decency and compassion."

---

[8] "The shepherd drives the wolf from the sheep's throat, for which the sheep thanks the shepherd as a liberator, while the wolf denounces him for the same act as the destroyer of liberty, especially since the sheep was a black one. Plainly the sheep and the wolf are not agreed upon a definition of the word 'liberty' and the same difference prevails amongst us human beings." Abraham Lincoln.

[9] George Bernard Shaw, *Getting Married* (New York: Macmillan, 1946), p. 38.

In one part of Arthur Koestler's book, *Thieves in the Night,* set in 1937, then Palestine, a small group of Jewish settlers are surrounded by a larger and better armed Arab force. The Arabs are intent on killing the Jews most of whom have fled from German death camps. During a temporary halt in the firing, one politically very liberal Jew asks another if he does not see the Arab point of view. The other replies "We cannot afford to see their point of view."[10]

And there are times when we cannot afford to give the opposite point of view as much validity as our own. If someone is intent on killing you, and is coming at you with a knife, and will not listen to anything you say, this is simply not the time to be concerned with the center of gravity of their worldview, what is most real to them, the injustices they suffered in childhood, or their ambitions for their children. It is simply time to prevent them from killing you, and hopefully doing this in a painful enough way that they will not be tempted to repeat the process at some later date.

The critical question for our ethical mandate is: Under what conditions do you ignore the other person's point of view? Justice Oliver Wendell Holmes provided part of the answer in his famous statement on constitutionally guaranteed liberties. He said: "Your right to wave your fist ends one inch from my nose."

This provides the basis for the answer to our critical question. The answer is that any individual, group, or species has the right to follow its own directives or whims, to succeed in its endeavors or to go to its own hell in its own ways, until its behavior comes threatening within one inch of our own nose, one foot of our children's noses,[11] one yard of the nose of the human race.

---

[10] Arthur Koestler, *Thieves in the Night* (New York: Macmillan, 1946), p. 38.

[11] "Our" children are all human children. A species that does not protect its young becomes extinct.

If we had read *Mein Kampf* before Hitler started his armies moving, we would have seen from his clear statements that he was within the limits of one inch from our nose and one foot from the children's noses. We would then have realized that we could not afford to be concerned with this point of view and stopped him quickly and easily at the Rhineland. The Iraqi attempted development of atomic weaponry, with a history of aggression whenever they thought they could get away with it. This was a clear violation of the one inch, one foot and one yard rule. (Any atomic war is a clear threat to the life of our species.) With the present proliferation of atomic weapons, one exploded bomb will lead to who knows where. One thing we know about war is that it leads to the unpredictable. And there are today certain surprises we cannot afford to risk. At a certain point of a disagreement if the Rule of Three is invaded, the threatened individual must become "unreasonable" in the sense that Edmund Cahn used the term. Negotiation ends, a flat viewpoint is taken, and the course of action must be taken. There is no further room for negotiation.[12] When protests to the world's governments failed, the Israelis took action and destroyed Iraq's nuclear capability.

The new ethical mandate is thus an extension of the philosopher John Stuart Mill's idea that each individual may only be controlled by society in order to stop him or her from doing harm to others. There are many difficult border areas here, ranging from abortion to drugs to the compulsory wearing of seat belts and crash helmets. In each of these the basic question is—"Is the behavior private or does it threaten others?" Some of these problems will need careful study of the individual cases. Others can be solved by direct application of the

---

[12] Herman Melville's story *Bartleby* is one illustration of the power of this "unreasonable" position. Melville well understood the importance of this point as illustrated by the failure of Starbuck in *Moby Dick* to take action at the proper time and thus save the Pequod and its crew.

rule. Thus consensual sex between adults is clearly their own business, but child abuse and the education of children is everybody's business. (All children are our children.) The actress Mrs. Patrick Campbell said she did not care what people did sexually "as long as they don't do it in the streets and frighten the horses"!

This ethical mandate has implications for many types of moral problems. Let us suppose that we learn that a helpless old person is secretly being kept prisoner and abused next door. Where does this guideline lead us? On first glance it appears that no part of the Rule of Three is invoked. We must simply let it go on as a private matter.

Looking more deeply, however, we see that we must take action under the one-inch rule. Each of us may be weak and helpless one day. In order to protect ourselves in this eventuality, in order to insure that *we* will be protected at that time, we must make sure that we live in a social climate where the old, the weak, and the helpless are protected and not exploited. This is like taking out accident insurance.

Unless there are basic rules to protect the weak and helpless humans, we are left open to the cold winds. We will if we live long enough be weak and helpless compared to someone else. The one-inch rule makes it imperative that we protect ourselves then by setting up the rules (take out the annuities—insurance policies) now.

We do not live only in a biological but also in a social environment and ecology. Both must be geared to nurture and protect us during the various stages of our life and prospering. Retirement insurance is one way. Equally necessary is the insurance of living in a society that by its rules provides social insurance. Public duties are an integral part of private self-protection.

If people believe that they can kill or exploit someone else for private gain or whim and not under the law, where does this leave *us* in the future? No matter how strong we are now, the future is uncertain and the ideas may be turned against us later and we are unprotected. "As the MacBeths found, such ideas cannot be kept in isolated compartments, they often spill over...."[13]

The situation is similar to that of boat and ship sailors. Unless we are watchful and responsive when others need help, we cannot expect it when we do. Unless the social system is such that you and everyone else is aware of, stops and helps those on a sinking ship, we will not be helped when our own ship is foundering. For our own protection we need a system that will protect those who have lost control of their own destiny, whether this loss is due to storm winds and high waves, age, incapacity, or more powerful and ruthless others.

A second aspect of this would be in the one-yard rule. We cannot expect there to be a protective attitude toward the human race if we see around us the weak and helpless members of the race being exploited. This gives a clear double message. If we wish the race to be protected, we must protect its members. That superb child psychiatrist Fritz Redl was once speaking to a group of parents. One asked how, in corrupt times like this, they could insure that their child developed a good and honest character. "There are three ways to do this," Redl replied. "Example, example, example."[14]

Or, as the psychoanalyst Helen Ross somewhere put it, "Attitudes are more caught than taught."[15]

We cannot go back to the classical Greek system of regarding as really human only adult, affluent, male citizens. Or the

---

[13] Mary Midgley, *Can't We Make Moral Judgements?* (New York: St. Martin's Press, 1991), p. 68.

[14] Fritz Redl, in a lecture at the New School for Social Research, New York City, 1947.

[15] Helen Ross, quoted in Caliandra Brum, *The Children of the Nineties* (New York: United Methodist Communications, 1991), p. 338.

Enlightenment view of only males. (The excellent educational system of Rousseau was only for boys.) Nor can we return to the Early American view of only male Caucasians. Nor to V.I. Lenin's, "What is moral is what is advantageous to the proletarian class."[16] Clearly all human beings is the smallest group we can be concerned about. The one-yard rule is the most complex of all. Either it is the whole human race or it does not cohere. The term and idea of "the family of man" is a truism and a dream. But it is a necessary goal if we wish to survive. We will be a family of man or our left-behind artifacts will be examined by the species that follows us as we examine the petrified footprints, bones, and eggs of the dinosaurs.

The American Indian Iroquois Six-Nation Confederacy was a democratic society which, for example, gave women an equal vote and political voice at a time when this was unknown in Western Europe, the Middle East, and Asia. It had as its Great Law, the *Haudenosaunee.* "In all our deliberations we must be mindful of the impact of our decisions on the seven generations to follow us."

We must, today, take this one step further if we wish to survive our knowledge of atomics and our growing knowledge of space travel. We must begin to say: "In all our deliberations we must be mindful of the impact of our decisions on the future survival of the human race."

If an old person is being abused and exploited behind locked doors, the social system that is necessary to protect me in the future has broken down. I must repair it or face the possible consequences.

In addition, if Group A militarily invades and takes over Group B, a social climate is produced in which we may be next. To protect ourselves and our children, we need to insure that

---

[16] V. I. Lenin, quoted in *Great Soviet Encyclopedia*, vol. 30 (New York: Macmillan, 1979), p. 338.

this is not done. We cannot say that Group A is simply following its own mores and should be left alone. We need insurance for our children that they will live in a climate that protects them from military invasion. Being in a strong military position oneself is not very much protection compared to a social climate. The French in 1938 believed themselves to have the strongest army in the world and to be secure behind the mightiest fortification line ever built. They—with the rest of the world—permitted the destruction of Ethiopia, Austria, Spain, Czechoslovakia, and a general climate of lawlessness. A few weeks in 1939 showed how weak a reed were their army and fortifications.

On the other hand, if Group A and Group B decide that they wish to batter each other and are stupid enough to settle disagreements with force, that is their affair unless atomic fallout is going to land on us or our children. Then, in John Stuart Mill's words "...the case is taken out of the province of liberty and placed in that of morality or law."[17]

A deer is attacked by wolves. Under the Rule of Three and its implications, I have no responsibility. I will never be a deer and neither will my children. There is no threat here to me, to human children, or to the human race. Unless I am competing with the wolves for food, there is no reason for me to act.

And when I do, it tends to backfire. We killed off the cougar who were preying on "the beautiful deer" in the Grand Canyon area of the Western United States. The deer multiplied since we disturbed the balance of nature, ate up all the local vegetation, changed the ecology of the area, and destroyed much of its life and deer-sustaining ability. In the barren landscape that resulted, they largely succumbed to illness and starvation.

---

[17] John S. Mill, quoted in Mary Midgley, *Can't We Make Moral Judgements?* (New York: St. Martin's Press, 1991), p. 44.

Thus from the viewpoint of this ethical guideline we actively interfere to protect the helpless person, who we ourselves may become in time, who is being abused next door. Further, child abuse, child prostitution, and forced suttee are public problems. Non-forced suttee with other viable options is a private matter. Abortion is a private matter. Selling drugs to children is of public concern. The education and development of children are public matters.

Although many cases must be decided on an individual case-by-case basis, the interpretation is often fairly obvious. Being drunk is a private affair. For a soldier, a physician, or a policeman to be drunk on duty is a public affair. Driving a car on public streets while drunk is a public matter. Suicide—except in the case of children—is a private matter.

In this view, as in that of John Stuart Mill, each individual may only be controlled by society in order to stop him from doing harm to others. "In the part [of his conduct] which merely concerns himself, his rule is, of right, absolute. Over himself, over his own body and mind, the individual is sovereign."[18]

The One Yard Rule has other implications. We face unknown problems of human survival in the future. What these will be, we cannot now even guess, except that they will be new and difficult. We may or may not be able to solve them, but to give us the best possible chance to do so we will need available all our resources in ability to think and to act. Any general procedure that reduces the amount of available intellectual or other ability lessens the probability of our being able to solve these problems and therefore to survive as a species. These procedures which reduce the probability of our surviving include social customs which prevent certain parts of the population from functioning at its highest level, its highest potential.

---

[18] John S. Mill, *On Liberty* (New York: Penguin, 1974), p. 136 (first published in 1859) .

Systematic discrimination against any race, other large group, or gender, prevents them from moving toward their potential and thereby reduces the overall ability of the human race to solve the new and as-yet-unimagined problems is lessened.

Therefore systematic discrimination against any sizable group of humans violates the one-yard rule and is everybody's problem.

It is impossible to predict what problems will arise in the future, what species-life or species-death conundrums we will face as we move forward in technology and outward in space. It is, therefore, equally impossible to predict what personality types we will need, what kinds of individual will be most adept when needed, most likely to be able to solve them. It is part of our need to survive as a race to offer as wide a latitude as possible to different personality types, to different developments of personality. This is true of both individuals and cultures, of persons, societies, and organizations. This, of course, is limited to those who do not run afoul of the one inch, one foot, one yard rule. Short of danger to ourselves and our children, we want and need as wide a variety of human personalities available as possible. "Mankind," wrote J.S. Mill, "are greater gainers by suffering each other to live as seems good to themselves than by compelling each to live as seem good to the rest."[19] Elsewhere Mill wrote: "...the only unfailing and permanent source of improvement is liberty, since by it there are as many possible sources of improvement as there are individuals."[20]

This is certainly not a new idea. Alexander von Humboldt in 1792, and Alexis de Toqueville in 1850, for example, pointed out that two things are necessary for human development, for growth in new directions, and flexibility in the face of adver-

---

[19] John S. Mill, *On Liberty*, p. 139.
[20] John S. Mill, *On Liberty*, p. 10.

sity. These two are freedom and a variety of personality structures, customs, beliefs, orientations. Today we would also use other descriptive phrases such as "ways of being in the world."

Censoring ideas, or art unless they run counter to the Rule of Three (and this can be, at least as far as children are concerned, a sticky point to be decided case by case where there are problems), is not public business. Censorship stultifies thought and growth. It makes for an orthodoxy that reduces individuality, and thereby makes less our resources for solving new and unprecedented problems. A concept is a tool and we cannot know what tools will be needed in the future. However, without available criticism of known ideas, they lose their strength and validity. They become schools instead of tools with sharp cutting edges. In Mill's words, "He who knows only his own side of the case knows little of that." Later he writes, "Both teachers and learners go to sleep at their post as soon as there is no enemy in sight."[21]

In particular, it is important to keep an atmosphere of freedom for ideas and for art. The artists help us see in new ways, to question our accepted views. They are not only the spearheads of new developments, they also sound the warning when our old views are paralyzing us. Like the canaries that miners used to take down into the mines to warn them of gas before they themselves could sense it, artists sound a signal when our customs and ways of viewing reality are preventing any movement. In the words of the artist Paul Klee: "The artist does not re roduce the visible; rather he makes things visible."[22] We humans tend to be much more one-sided than many-sided. To remain viable in the unpredictable future, we need many different kinds of individuals and different kinds of living ideas.

---

[21] John S. Mill, *On Liberty*, p. 136.
[22] Paul Klee, quoted in H. B. Chipp, *Theories of Modern Art* (Berkeley: University of California Press, 1956), p. 182.

Art being free is everyone's concern. All that is needed is an absence of censorship. It is everyone's business to see that art is not censored, but it is not everyone's business to support it. It is no one else's business how the artists make their living, just that they are not prevented. In the art field, the opposite of Gresham's Law operates—eventually good art drives out bad art. A Van Gogh or a Mozart may starve to death in the meantime, but it is their business how they spend their lives. The important factor in all of this is to prevent any type of national or supranational censorship.

The "purpose" of art is defined by the artist. One—as Victor Hugo—may believe it should stimulate and record progress. Another—as Charles Dickens—that it should serve humanity. Another—like Baudelaire—that art should be simply for its own sake. However, for a society to be fertile and have new perceptions and ideas, to be able to move toward its own potentialities, its artists must be free. It is usually the artist who teach us new ways of thinking and being in the world, as the Impressionists opened the way for modern physics and modern psychodynamics. They taught us to think in ways which would go below the surface of things. Since 1870, painting has become less and less an attempt to reproduce on canvas the way three-dimensional objects appear to the human eye, and more and more an attempt to examine their inner uniqueness and flow, and their relation to the eye of the specific artist. From this to Freudian dynamics, Relativity theory and Quantum Mechanics is a straight path.

Hopefully there will always be among human beings a great cultural diversity with many different standards of good and bad, right and wrong. Hopefully also there will be much flux and development. And these futures are, in principle, unpredictable. We cannot tell in advance how a culture will develop, what ideas it will consider valid or invalid, what new concepts it will develop, how it will construe reality, or even what clothes it will consider correct, what potential foods it will consider edible or inedible, who it will approve of having sexual relations with whom, and thousands of other similar variables. The diversity will not only be between cultures, but inside many of them. The United States at this time, for example, has Quakers and Amish, and a popularity of incredibly violent "Rambo" movies, elects idealists, actors, and ex-CIA heads as presidents, reads widely the *National Enquirer,* supports Public Radio and TV, listens to both AM and FM radio, is vitally interested and concerned about one child who falls down a well and uninterested in many thousands of children slowly starving to death, calls the 900 psychic hotline, supports NASA, and generally speaking is as diverse in as many areas as you can think of.

It, however, is not all diversity. There may be no constant point in physical space (Einstein once described the Theory of Relativity by saying, "There is no hitching post in the universe"), but this is not true in the human universe. There is one point we humans can all agree on, one hitching post among our diverse desires. We want the human race to continue to exist. It is on this "desired outcome" that the present ethical guideline is built. What cultural patterns we would like to exist in the future, on this we differ, but on the existence itself we agree.

It may well be true, as Spinoza wrote, that "Nature has no fixed end in view," but we humans do. We want to continue our individual existence, the existence of our children and that of our species for as long as possible under the best possible conditions. It may not be "Nature's" goal, but it is ours.

I write in this book, as, being who I am, I must, for the Western mind. For an Eastern desire and goal for all sentient beings to give up their physical form and to be "released from the Wheel of Things" (the long cycle of reincarnation), I cannot speak as I do not comprehend. I can only wonder.

So far I have written as if all actions could be judged as either public or private; as of concern to all of us, or of concern only to the person performing the action. However, there is a third class of actions that might be termed "contract" actions. The ethical judgment as to how to behave is made in terms of an implicit or explicit contract between the individual and the community involved. One example of an implicit contract of this sort is the generally accepted legal principle, "Ignorance of the law is no excuse." There is an implicit contract to the effect that the individual is expected to know the law of the community in which he or she is functioning.[23]

Thus if there is a law in a community that seat belts are to be worn when in a car, the community would have no responsibility for you if you were injured in an accident while not wearing them. Not even the responsibility to send ambulances or provide medical care. Similarly if there were a rule concerning motorcycles and crash helmets, and you became paralyzed for life in a crash while not wearing one, the community would have no responsibility for giving you the care you would need to remain alive. (Whether or not personal insurance would cover you in these cases would depend on what is in the explicit contract between you and the insurance company.)

The rules about exhaust emissions for your car are in a different class. These concern the one inch and one foot rule (fist-waving rights in front of our noses and those of our children) and would be treated as such. The community would act in such a way as to prevent violations from continuing and do it in such a way as to have a positive effect on violation behavior on the part of others.

The approach to ethics presented here strongly implies personal responsibility for one's actions. Except in special cases

---

[23] I am indebted to Louise Moed, Attorney-at-Law, for clarification on this point.

such as feeblemindedness and brain damage, each adult is held accountable for what he or she does. (Children are to be protected and educated, not judged.) Extenuating circumstances will frequently exist, and must in any human-oriented society (a society where the human being is more real than the law) be taken into account on a case by case basis. However, every individual adult is held to be responsible for his actions and accounted to have done them voluntarily.

Perhaps the silliest argument in all of philosophy or psychology (and that takes *some* doing!) is the one over freedom of the will. In all the discussions no one among the advocates has ever said that he or she was not free to discuss the issue and come to an intelligent free will answer to the problem. Others might be completely determined and have no free will— the speaker was always free. And, of course, the speaker had to come to this decision. To decide that we, ourselves, have no freedom of thought is madness. Determinism means an end to all hope or joy. At best, it leaves us in a "romantic mood of resignation." It also means an end to all ethics and moral judgements. It also leads to an end of all meaningful and social intercourse and an insanity in which we believe and feel that we use our will to deny the existence of our will. Discussion of determinism is, as Santayana says somewhere, "pure conversation." John Austin wrote:

> They all *talk* about determinism and *say* they believe in it. I've never met a determinist in my life. I mean a man who really believes in it as you and I believe that men are mortal. Have you?[24]

To paraphrase Schopenhauer, determinism does not need a refutation, but a cure.

---

[24] John Austin, quoted in Roger Hawsheer in his Introduction to Isaiah Berlin's *Against the Current* (New York: Penguin, 1979).

I have not discussed the ethics of the Existentialist schools and philosophers such as Jaspers, Heidegger, or Sartre. This is such a complex movement with so many diverse elements that it is hard to find a single "ethic" that runs through it. The emphasis is on "choosing," of making decisions, and thereby bringing oneself into fuller existence. Insofar as I follow it, any objective set of ethical rules violates the ability to choose. Ethical theory is therefore, in itself, morally bad. It is seen as an attempt to escape from freedom by hiding behind a set of rules, whether these rules are seen as the laws of the universe or as reasonable hypotheses. The only evil that philosophers who call themselves Existentialists appear to agree on is that of avoiding one's existence by acting unauthentically. Most of these philosophers have led lives we would consider to be highly moral by most present-day Western standards. Some have not. Some, like Heidegger, have been Nazis. Either of these courses seems equally valid from the basic structure of Existentialist theory.

The Existentialist urges us to be constantly aware of our subjectivity and that any attempt to set up objective standards of morality is doomed to failure since it is an evasion—an evasion of our highly individual, subjective, unique state. Given this as truth, there can be no standard for distinguishing right from wrong except "authenticity."

However, a search of our "subjectivity" reveals at least one common factor, common to individuals who are sane by any cultural standards except perhaps that of Thuggee. This common factor is the deep desire that the cosmos be not empty of human life. This does lead, today, to a set of standards for behavior.

The Rule of Three (one inch, one foot, one yard) also indicates the relative importance of survival for ourselves, our children and our species. From this viewpoint there is the clear implication that—if it comes to a choice—the self must be sacrificed for the children, and the self and the children for the human race. The choice will come rarely, but when it does it cannot be escaped. "If I knew something useful to my nation, but ruinous to another nation, I would not propose it to my ruler, because I am a man before I am a Frenchman, or rather because I am a man by necessity and a Frenchman only by chance of birth....If I knew something useful to my country, but prejudicial to Europe, or useful to Europe but prejudicial to the human race, I would consider it a crime." [25] From time to time a human being is asked to stand and die at his or her Thermopalae. It is not only the tree of liberty that needs blood to nourish it from time to time, it is also the tree of human survival itself.

---

[25] Montesquieu, *Les Philosophes*, Norman Torrey, ed. (New York: Capricorn Books, 1960).

CHAPTER SEVEN

THE PROBLEM OF RADICAL EVIL

If a way to the better there be, it lies in taking a full look at the worst.

—Thomas Hood

In 1793, the philosopher Immanuel Kant wrote a strange and disturbing essay. We are just beginning to realize the implications of this work. Only since the new physics of Planck and Einstein can we see deeper into the problem than was possible for Kant. Only since the Holocaust can we really begin to comprehend the reality of the problem. Only since the atomic bomb can we begin to know its terrible relevance for us today.

Kant's essay, "Religion Within the Limits of Reason Alone," set out to look at a particular kind of human behavior which he called "Radical Evil."[1] To him, radical evil refers to a kind of action so terrible that it overwhelms our ability to think about it consistently in our usual frame of reference; is irrelevant to our usual system of law. Literally our legal system cannot deal with it in meaningful terms. About all we can do is call the perpetuator a "monster," not human, and kill him or it. In this context it is of interest to note that the majority of letters to the government of Israel, and to the newspapers, protesting the execution of Adolf Eichmann did so on the grounds that his actions were so terrible that the death sentence was irrelevant and therefore not a fitting punishment.[2] Hannah Arendt has pointed out that the "true hallmark of Radical Evil about whose nature so little is known" is that we do not know how to punish these offenses or to forgive them. They "transcend the realm of human affairs and the potentiality of human power, both of whom they destroy when they make their appearance."[3]

Kant wrote that actions defined as radical evil destroy all our "maxims," and the ground on which they were developed. This refers to the fact that we each live by certain "maxims," rules put in general statements such as "do unto others," "the affairs of my family always come before the needs of others," "your good name is your most important asset," "always tell the truth," "enrich yourself by any means," "take care of yourself first because that is what everyone does and it is the only way to survive," "protect the weaker ones," "seize the moment," "obey the law," and so forth. Each of these general rules comes out of—and is a reasonable and logical result of—a particular view of reality and how it functions (in Kant's terms, the

---

[1] Immanuel Kant, "Religion Within the Limits of Reason Alone," in *Kant's Theory of Ethics*, 4th ed. (London: Longman Green, 1899), pp. 9 ff.

[2] Hannah Arendt, *Eichmann in Jerusalem* (New York: Viking, 1963), p. 228.

[3] Hannah Arendt, quoted in Jonathan Schell, *The Fate of the Earth*, (New York: Knopf, 1982).

"ground" from which they were developed). Each of us has a general "story" as to what the world is like, and has developed a set of "maxims" as to how we should behave. (The poet Muriel Rukeyser wrote, "The world is made up of stories, not of atoms.") If our basic maxim is "Everyone is for himself only," and we see someone who behaves otherwise, we can say of him, "Of course it is true that every person has a price, but they just have not offered it yet or else we just don't know where the secret safe deposit box is." In the extreme case of contradiction, we can say, "It is the exception that proves the rule," and go on with our belief strengthened by an observation pointing in the opposite direction.

However, there are some observations that simply cannot be fitted into any story, any narrative about how-the-world-works in which human beings could live. In what sort of story, for example, could we fit Ilse Koch's special barracks at Buchenwald Concentration Camp where all pregnant women prisoners were confined? They were each given triple the usual food rations in order to preserve their strength and make their dying longer. When they came to delivery, they were taken to an open space in the center of the camp, their ankles were chained closely together, and they were left alone to die in the agony of being unable to give birth.

This is radical evil. In what kind of story of reality does it fit? Perhaps in one of complete chaos or one run by the devil. But these are not universes that human beings can live in and survive as human. The actions of Ilse Koch rupture all our pictures of how-the-world-works. It can fit in none of them. Nor can our systems of jurisprudence encompass them; no punishment we can conceive is just. Nor can we find a way to forgive them.

Radical evil does not, today, have an explanation. It exists, and we see human beings, including ourselves, turn, as Kant wrote, against our own best interests. It is "as if each of us carries a malevolent stowaway that could come to life at any moment without cause or explanation."[4] Ibsen put it, "We are sailing with a corpse in our cargo."[5] Our systems of explanation do not deal with it any more than our systems of jurisprudence cover it. We simply cannot design a world in which humans can live which includes it. Ivan Karamazov makes this point to Alyosha when he described a 5-year-old girl who was tortured by her parents, forced to sleep in a cold privy, who had her mouth repeatedly filled with excrement. How can you believe in a God-filled world, or a God, when this happens, Ivan asks. Alyosha has no answer, nor do we.

Earlier philosophers, such as Plato, had blamed evil on ignorance. Kant's view was that actions such as this were not due to ignorance of what one should do, but were due to deliberate acts of will, and overcame the ground on which our maxims were built, preventing us from developing new ones. Today we would translate this into the concept that there is no way we could construe reality, no way in which we could live, that would include such actions. Literally in the presence of radical evil we are forced to the knowledge that the world, as we know it, contains elements which it cannot hold. We must live in an ordered universe or we have no basis for rules for our perceptions, feelings, belief, and actions. Radical evil destroys the order of the cosmos and threatens us with living in chaos. Without rules for determining if our perceptions are real, our feelings valid, our actions relevant to the situation, our decisions correct in terms of our goals, we cannot survive. And in a universe of chaos, or one run by the devil (the "Father of Lies"), there are no such rules.

---

[4] Gordon E. Michalson, *Fallen Freedom* (Cambridge: Cambridge University Press, 1990), p. x.

[5] Ibsen, quoted in Gorden E. Michalson, *Fallen Freedom*, p. 29.

This translation of Kant's formulation is part of the legacy of the Planck and Einstein contributions to modern thought. They demonstrated that we construe reality in different ways at different times for different purposes. There is, they showed, no way to know what "reality" really is because there is not even a theoretical way to observe it before it is profoundly alloyed with our consciousness. Science no longer searches for the "truth" about reality, but for the most useful ways to construe it. We can no more decide which is the "true" construction of reality than we can decide which is the "true" shape of the clay from which we have fashioned the cup, the plate, the vase, or the work of art.

Kant had elsewhere first pointed this out, but it was the physicists who developed it, due to the necessity they found of finding different systems of explanation for the phenomena in the too-small-to-see-even-theoretically (the Quantum universe), phenomena theoretically at least within the range of sight and touch (the Neutonian universe), and phenomena too-large-or-fast-to-see-even-theoretically (the Relativity universe). These universes, or ways of construing reality, each have their own laws and basic limiting principles. In the Quantum way of construing reality—for example, cause and effect—are replaced by statistical causation. In the Relativity universe, time and space cannot be meaningfully separated. These universes are very different from each other, but not mutually contradictory.

How do we human beings behave in the presence of radical evil? Our minds find it very hard to deal with, and skitter away from perceiving, accepting, or remembering it. In 1993, for example, 22 percent of Americans believed that the Holocaust probably did not happen, and 12 percent believed that it could not have happened.[6] This is one out of five Americans. What would we say if one out of five Americans did not believe that the Civil War ever happened, and 12 percent believed that it could not have happened? Or that the same figures applied to the existence of President Roosevelt? How have we behaved in the face of the existence of the hydrogen bomb, with its possibility of destroying all life on our only planet? At the very least, our behavior has been far from rational. George F. Kennan, our former ambassador to Russia and an outstanding expert on international relations, wrote:

> We have gone on piling weapon upon weapon, missile upon missile, new levels of destruction upon old ones, helplessly, almost involuntarily like victims of some sort of hypnotism, like men in a dream, like lemmings headed for the sea.[7]

Or in Einstein's words:

> The public, having been warned of the horrible nature of atomic warfare, has done nothing about it and to a large extent has dismissed the warning from its consciousness.[8]

The psychiatrist Kurt Goldstein described what he called Catastrophic Anxiety. This is a terribly distressing and painful fear that our very being, our entire mental apparatus, is about to fly apart, to fall into innumerable pieces. It comes about because we have built our mental apparatus upon our idea of how the world is and works: upon a *Weltbild*, a world picture. This picture of reality, and our mental structure, mutually support each

---

[6] Roper Poll, *New York Times*, Aug. 30, 1993, p. 1.

[7] Quoted in Edward M. Kennedy and Mark O. Hatfield, *Freeze! How You Can Help Prevent Nuclear War* (New York: Bantam, 1982), p. 98.

[8] *Freeze! How You Can Help Prevent Nuclear War,* p. 68.

other and each is dependent on the other for its coherence and organization. When a perception that we cannot deny cannot fit in the world picture we use, it destroys our belief in the validity of the picture. Our mental apparatus then loses its supports and is threatened with disintegration. A terrible and deep anxiety results. We will do almost anything to end this anxiety, and this includes all our powers of denial to avoid the impact of the perception. We deny in one way or another the perception and/or its importance. We know that the threat to our personality is real and must be dealt with. We know that with no support system from outside that the mental structure which is our existence cannot continue to function. We act with all our ability and techniques to remove the threat by denying its reality, or its importance.

One of the best ways to deny the reality of a problem is to do nothing about it. The doing nothing strengthens our feeling that there is no real problem.

The same data has been seen in the field of anthropology. In this field there were observations of people who were raised in one culture with its specific coherent view of reality. Then another stronger culture destroyed theirs, or else they were removed from their home society and taken into another with a very different view of reality, a very different story of how the world worked. Very frequently these people had no sense of any purpose for their lives, a general rootlessness, and a great deal of self-destructive behavior. In anthropology they were called "Marginal Men." One frequently observed example of this were many of the individuals raised in the Plains Indian culture shortly before this was destroyed by the white society taking over their living areas.

In the face of radical evil, unable to fit the observations made into any coherent picture of the world, unable to bear the dissonance of it in our usual world picture, unable to construct a viable-for-humans world picture in which it would fit, terribly threatened with catastrophic anxiety, the mind slips away from—denies—the perception. The searchlight of our consciousness, illuminating first one thing and then another circles around this, does not perceive it, does not deal with it. Somehow it seems not true, not real. The same perception is there, but no longer real and observed. Any sane bombardier in World War II would have been as horrified and sick at seeing a row of babies he had just incinerated as Eichmann became on seeing a truckload of Jews being gassed to death. (Eichmann had to run away and throw up in horror.) Then with the same sort of psychological mechanisms, both would get on with their tasks of incinerating and gassing from a distance, in a highly organized manner and with a concern for doing a good job in a good cause, and with a complete denial that they were engaging in radical evil, or that there was any present that was being done by their side.

The ultimate radical evil action which would not fit in any narrative of how the world works in which humans could survive, is action leading to the destruction of the human species. We might kill individuals, wreck societies, destroy entire cultures; somewhere still is the possibility of a meaningful, viable construction of reality. At the bottom of Pandora's box lay hope. But if there are no humans left alive, if our species is destroyed, hope also dies. No possibility of meaning then exists for us. The planet may continue to spin, but it does so without meaning and value.

Most of us manage to avoid the radical evil that has been around us the past years as we observe the population of Earth moving steadily toward the point where life cannot be sup-

ported. We hear over and over of the rain forests being cut
down, and the oceans poisoned, that our supply of oxygen is
at mortal threat. We have permitted the growth of the world's
supply of atomic weapons to grow and grow beyond all possible sanity. Even those few who can face the problem of possible human extinction seem unable to comprehend why others
cannot. Paul and Anne Erlich, who have tried very hard to make
the general public aware of the danger of annihilation of the
human species, called a chapter of their important book, *The
Population Explosion,*[9] "Why Isn't Everyone As Frightened
As We Are?" Alas! they have no answer to this crucial question.

In October, 1951, the editors of *Colliers Magazine* brought
out a special issue of 125 pages called "Preview of the War We
Do Not Want." The editors stated that they believed it to be
the most important issue that any magazine has ever published.
Plans were complete to publish it as a book. The contributors
included Hanson Baldwin, Stuart Chase, Edward R. Murrow,
Marguerite Higgins, J.B. Priestly, Walter Reuther, Philip Wylie,
Robert Sherwood, and others. The reaction was tremendous
and almost entirely negative. It resulted in a storm of protest.

> So much that the editors hurriedly dropped the project
> of its republication in book form. The reaction was typi-
> cal of the public's passionate rejection of any warning
> which brings out people's repressed fears and compels
> them to to face, if even for an instant, the hideous and
> threatening reality around them.[10]

Generally speaking one does not talk about questions of
species survival. To bring them up is gauche—people respond

[9] Paul R. Erlich and Anne H. Erlich, *The Population Explosion* (New
York: Simon & Schuster, 1990).
[10] Arthur Koestler, *The Trail of the Dinosaur* (New York: Macmillan,
1956), p. 148.

with a somewhat embarrassed air and change the subject as soon as possible. It is made plain that you have brought up a subject not discussed in this group. It is not taboo exactly, just not done. Keep bringing it up and you will find yourself outside the group.

Behind this is the knowledge that it is not only radical evil to so act as to increase the likelihood of the end of the existence of our species, it is also radical evil to acquiesce in that action. All of us know the truth of the old wisdom that the only thing necessary for evil to triumph is for good men and women to do nothing. We all know that to the degree we have not seized every opportunity to protest and scream, to the degree we have not been involved in the efforts to save our planet and species; to the degree we have ignored the warnings, we have been acquiescing. And to that degree, we have been guilty of radical evil.

And clearly we have acquiesced in, been a part of, radical evil. When we had atomic weapons equal to 600 Hiroshima-sized bombs, when we and the Russians could easily have ended all life on Earth in a war, all sat back as we went on designing larger bombs, and intelligent people rationalized this in words well-suited to the theater of the absurd. *The Washington Star* reported on March 4, 1962:

> Harry S. Truman said today President Kennedy is on the right track in his decision to resume atomic atmospheric testing. It was the right thing to do. We should never have stopped. Where would we be today if Thomas Edison had been forced to stop his experiment with the electric light bulb? [11]

---

[11] Quoted in Norman Corwin, *Overkill and Megalove* (New York: World Publ. Co., 1963), p. 23.

After it was publicly known that radioactive traces of our testing could be found everywhere on Earth, that Japanese fishermen over 120 miles from a test had died of radioactive poisoning, and that our air, water, and food supplies were menaced, Admiral Strauss, head of the Atomic Energy Commission, set up a special educational program to assure the world that there was no real danger. He called this program "Operation Sunshine." [12]

A chapter like this faces a tremendous uphill task. It must early on remind people of something that they do not want to be reminded of, and usually will *not* be reminded of. It must bring up a subject that people usually avoid, or deal with at as much distance as they can. The subject is doubly damned and doubly to be avoided. It is that radical evil exists on a large scale today, and we have been guilty of it.

Since 1945 and certainly since the advent of the hydrogen bomb, we have known that the survival of our species was at risk. Since then information on the gradual wrecking of our oxygen supply through the poisoning of the oceans and the cutting down of the rain forests has repeatedly come through to us. We can no longer plead ignorance. There have been enough pleas from hardworking, but small and inadequate organizations such as Greenpeace, The Environmental Defense Fund, and others, for our help, which we have ignored so that we cannot even plead helplessness. Our lack of action and involvement is, itself, an act of will. It is so hard to face the existence of radical evil when done by others, how much harder it is to face it in ourselves; when done and acquiesced in by ourselves? And yet a book like this, hoping to make some positive

---

[12] Robert K. Jung, *Brighter Than a Thousand Suns* (New York: Harcourt Brace, 1950), p. 312.

change for the future, to give a tiny push in the direction of saving our human species, must make this point if only by unavoidable implication. Unless we realize our culpability, how can we learn to behave in less culpable ways? As part of our system of denial, there is a strong tendency not to read, or to ignore the implications of, books such as *The Population Explosion, Brighter Than a Thousand Suns,* Edward Kennedy and Mark Hatfield's excellent action handbook *Freeze: How You Can Help Prevent Nuclear War,* or this chapter.

CHAPTER EIGHT

EDUCATION
FOR A NEW AGE

Human history becomes more and more a race between
education and catastrophe.

—H. G. Wells

It is clear that a new system of education is needed for the new
age we have now entered. The purpose of an educational system is to enable our children to survive the environment in
which they will live. That environment changed radically on
the day that the first atomic bomb was dropped, and again on
the day Neil Armstrong stepped onto the Moon.

To change a system of education is a very difficult and ex-
pensive thing to do. However, the cost in effort and money
must, as in all other transactions, be measured against what
we are trying to accomplish. Just as in the interaction of nations, those that are not willing to pay the cost of peace must
pay the cost of war, so in the survival of the human race, if we

are not willing to pay the price of survival, we face the risk of extermination.

The system of education described in the following pages rests on the psychological knowledge which we now have concerning what the individual needs if he or she is to grow up as a citizen who lives with zest and enthusiasm, one who is protective of himself, the local community, and the human race. It will be based on five tracks that each child will be on from the very beginning of his or her formal educational experience.[1] These will be kept clear and conscious by both teachers and students at all levels.

1. To accept, value, use, express, and celebrate oneself as a unique individual.
2. To accept, value, use, express and celebrate oneself as a member of one's local community, to contribute to it in the ways best suited to the synthesis between its needs and one's individual personality.
3. To feel at home in other constructions of reality. Finding one's best ways to feel a part of the larger community of all human life, all sentient life, or the cosmos itself.
4. To attain certain basic skills needed to live and prosper in one's society.
5. To learn how to learn. To find the ways in which you as an individual learn best.

These are placed in this order for good reasons. To accomplish the second and third well and healthily depends (as all modern psychology teaches us) on a healthy development of the first.

---

[1] In this educational system, there is much less new than meets the eye. It owes great debts to Johann Pestalozzi, Friedrich Froebel, John Dewey, and other such giants.

(Lewis Mumford wrote in this context: "To be on friendly terms with every part of mankind, one must be on equally friendly terms with every part of oneself...").[2] The fourth and fifth tracks will usually be accomplished in the course of the first three.

Although the concept of the five tracks will be kept clear and conscious, in practice there will be a good deal of overlap. A specific activity may well be on both tracks one and three, for example.

If we wish to break down these five tracks even further, we would say that the two basic goals of this kind of education are clarification of experience and the establishment of self-esteem. Understanding our own response to our experiences, we can find the kinds of activities for which we are individually suited and which therefore give us zest and enthusiasm when we engage in them. This participation in our natural ways of being, relating, creating, leads us to a sense of self-worth as individual, as a part of our immediate community and as a part of the community of humankind. Essentially learning is seen as a process of becoming, and the educational institution is a facilitator for individuals to develop in their own unique directions. This concept has been elaborated in a number of books and papers such as those by Edgar Z. Friedenberg, John C. Esty, and Eda LeShan.[3]

  1. To accept, value, use, express, and celebrate oneself as a unique individual.

---

[2] Lewis Mumford, *The Transformations of Man* (New York: Harper & Bros., 1956), p. 188.

[3] Edgar Z. Friedenberg, *The Vanishing Adolescent* (New York: Dell Paperback, 1962); John C. Esty, "The Lamp of Learning, Not the Shoehorn," in Frederick Raubinger and Harold Rowe, *The Individual and Education* (New York: Macmillan, 1968); Eda J. LeShan, *The Conspiracy Against Childhood* (New York: Antheneum, 1968).

This track will be concerned with the question for each student: "What kinds of activity fill me with enthusiasm, turn me on, do I really enjoy and get lost in so when I look up from them I feel good, relaxed and with a good tired feeling? At this level of my development what can I do to celebrate and use my uniqueness? In what way am I most like myself (as opposed to being most like others)? What activities 'sing me' as an individual? What kinds of activity make me the best company for myself? What do I need in the ways of special skills and knowledge to get the most out of these?"

Students at each age level will be presented with a wide variety of possible activities and encouraged to choose one or more by means of these criteria. The encouragement of students' individuality will be a very powerful factor in reducing intrapersonal stresses now and later. No matter what theoretical viewpoint we hold concerning the human psyche, recognition and encouragement of this sort can only be seen as an aid to health.

2. To accept, value, use, express, and celebrate oneself as a member of one's local community.

The basic question of this track is: "What aspects of group activity can I participate in with more enthusiasm? What expresses and celebrates me as a member of the present social group with which I primarily identify (class, school, community, country)? What activities of the group can I engage in that I enjoy, and which contribute to the group? In what ways am I most like other members of my group? What can I do to strengthen the integration of the group and therefore my sense of belonging to it? What do I need in the way of special skills and knowledge to do this most fully?" As John Dewey pointed out so clearly, genuine individuality is impossible unless the person is a sustained and sustaining part of a social whole.[4]

---

[4] John Dewey. See, for example, *Reconstruction in Philosophy* (Boston: Beacon Press, 1948).

At each developmental period of the specific individual, and at each age group generally, various possibilities will be presented—if they do not suggest themselves—to the members of the group. These will range over as wide a spectrum as possible, including such possibilities as sports, theater, dance, choral activities, community service, record-keeping, researching new ideas and directions for the group, housekeeping, etc.[5]

3. To feel at home in other constructions of reality.

There are two basic questions on this track. The first question is: "What celebrates and expresses me as a member of the human race? What activities can I engage in that will affirm me and also affirm my being part of something larger than myself, my immediate family, and local group? How am I most like all other human beings?" This is the basic approach to the Unitary Reality construction of reality. At each age, appropriate activities will be introduced as possibilities ranging from UNICEF fundraising, study of other cultures (different ways of being at home in the world), peace and ecology activities, meditation procedures leading to cosmic consciousness experience, etc.

The second question is: "In what other constructions of reality such those found in art forms, play, prayer, etc. can I engage and participate? This is done only for the sake of my own enjoyment and growth and with no practical value." This is presented as necessary for the growth and health of the individual, and any individual who does not have a way or ways to express the mythic construction of reality fully and joyfully (and wishes he or she had more time to devote to this), is regarded as we would regard a person who has a vitamin deficiency: that this is a potentially dangerous lack that needs active steps taken to deal with it.

---

[5] As Justice Holmes somewhere wrote: "A man should share the actions and passions of his times at perils of being judged not to have lived."

4. To attain basic skills needed to live and prosper in one's
   society.

An overall list would be made of the skills and the knowledge
needed to survive and function well in the particular society in
which the individual lives. This would be maintained and up-
dated every so often. Skills and knowledge areas would be classified by very general age groupings, such as "prepubertal,"
"late adolescence," "young adulthood," etc. Most of these would
be "picked up" by the students in their attempts to work on
Tracks 1, 2, and 3. This list would include such abilities as being able to make change, read, balance a checkbook, listen to
and evaluate people running for public office and voting with
care, looking up new information, being able to present one's
ideas and point of view, parent a child, retrieve information
from a computer, personal hygiene, drive a car, work cooperatively in a group, work alone, know some of the great lessons
and questions of history, and so forth.

When a student's file shows that he or she has not picked
up one of these areas at an appropriate age, it will be included
in the individual curriculum designed—and redesigned from
time to time for this person.

The basic skills needed to function and prosper vary mark-
edly according to the society in which people are raised. In
Bali it is necessary that everyone learns to dance; among the
Senoi everyone should be able to interpret dreams; in the United
States everyone must learn to read and do basic arithmetic.
Culture, wrote the sociologist Max Weber, consists of those
things which an individual must know in order to function as
one of its members. Without a culture the person barely, if at
all, exists. The best way to destroy a culture is to force it to
teach its children what some other culture considers essential,
and not the skills that fall within its own definition. This pro-
duces a class of individuals that the anthropologists have called

"marginal men," people with no firm footing in any coherent cultural system. Almost invariably these people have weak and fragile personality structures, lack goals in life, and are prone to self-destructive behaviors. With no firm footing in a cultural system with its grounding in a clear definition of reality, they are at best rootless, vulnerable, and ineffective people.

5. To learn how to learn.

As each new activity on Tracks 1, 2, 3, and 4 is experimented with, the teacher will help the student to move into it, to see what is needed in the way of knowledge and skills to do it with more zest, completion and satisfaction, and how to get these skills. The experience of learning, and learning how to learn, would be built into the system through experience in the students' development in his or her own way as a unique individual, as a member of a local group, as a participant in the human community, and in becoming comfortable with other ways of construing reality.

In this educational system, we follow the great dictum of the mining engineer and sociologist Frederic Le Play—that the most important product that comes out of the mine is the miner.[6] The goal of an educational system is the person who comes out of it, not statistics on mathematical ability, or test passing and failing. The question is, "What kind of human beings are coming out of the pipeline? How do they see reality and react to it? Do they care about others? Do they have zest and enthusiasm for their lives? Are they the kind of human beings you feel good

---

[6] Frederic Le Play, quoted in Lewis Mumford, *The Transformations of Man* (New York: Harper & Bros., 1956), p. 241.

about sharing the planet with? Are they all alike or is there
great diversity? Do they believe in the rights of others to march
to different drummers?"[7]

Unfortunately most late 20th-century education (which has
long forgotten the lessons of Froebel and Dewey) seems more
concerned with the figures that come out of the educational
system than it does with the individuals. The concern is not
with self-esteem and with the clarification of experience, but
with group reading levels and the percentage of students passing examinations. These exams determine who gets where in
the next level; who gets into what school or college when they
leave the present one. Indeed, it might be fairly stated that
most students get into an educational institution in order to
get out of it well, rather than to learn, grow and develop in it.

One problem for people raised in an educational institution with this orientation is they tend to learn to trust figures,
statistics, and other authorities more than they do their own
experience. The legal theorist, Edmund Cahn, tells the story
of the Chinese peasant who decided to buy a pair of shoes to
cover his bare feet. He carefully measured them and then set
out to walk to the town where there was a shoe store. When he
got there he found he had forgotten the measurements and
turned back to walk the long miles homeward to get them. When
asked why he could not determine the correct size by trying
shoes on his bare feet, he replied, "I trust the measurements
more than I do the feet."[8]

[7] Loren Eiseley wrote: "The special value of science lies not in what it
makes of the world, but what it makes of the knower," in *The Firma-
ment of Time* (New York: Atheneum, 1960), p. 173.
[8] Edmund Cahn, *The Moral Decision* (Bloomington, IN: Indiana University Press, 1955), p. 38.

This education system would not turn students into helpless, exploitable pacifists. The first and second track would prevent this. They would know the truth of Archibald MacLeish's statement: "If you turn the other cheek to a Fascist you get your head knocked off."[9] It would, however, develop citizens who had no inner need to go to war, citizens to whom war would be acceptable if necessary, but not tempting. It would develop human beings who were protective of themselves, their families, and the human race; humans who were fit to live in the new age we have entered, and who could survive and prosper among the stars.

It is easy to say that these ideas are not practical. This statement has governed a good deal of our decision-making process. Unless, however, we redefine the word practical our present troubles will increase and end us all. In *The New York Times* (March 15, 1970), the architecture critic Ada Louise Huxtable wrote:

> ...one practical decision after another has led us to the brink of cosmic disaster and there we sit, in pollution and chaos, courting the end of the earth. Just how practical can you get?

---

[9] Quoted in E. T. Hall, *Beyond Culture* (New York: Doubleday, 1971), p. 213.

CHAPTER NINE

HOW TO TEACH ETHICAL BEHAVIOR TO OUR CHILDREN: A PLACE TO BEGIN

Regarded as though from outer space or another dimension in time, human history presents a spectacle of repeated failures of great ideas to penetrate the human heart.

—Jacob Needleman

In the previous chapter I described the kind of educational system that we will need if we wish to survive the age of atomics and space. There is little really new in what I wrote there and in what I am writing in this appendix. Many educators have long been aware of, and have worked for, the kind of approach I am describing. The only aspect that is new is my relating these ideas to the central idea of this book—the change in the human situation since August 6, 1945.

It is an ambitious program. It calls for a complete change in our educational system. In that sense, it is indeed "Utopian Engineering" with all the disadvantages which inevitably accompany that approach. This is not a program to be put into place overnight in a sweeping revolution. It is only too clear from history that revolutionary changes, put into effect all at once, lead only to disaster. Whatever we do, if we wish it to be successful, must be done one step at a time. In the following pages are some comments on the first of these we must take.

The first step in raising and educating children who will have a good chance to keep our race alive in the next period of our history is for us to recognize as critical that children need to feel safe. Unless they feel this way, all our efforts to save our species are likely to fail. So long as we continue to betray this need, children will grow up to be damaged adults who cannot fully care for themselves, others, or the human race.

Children must have two things in order to feel safe. First, they must know that adults care enough for them to be actively working for their safety. The goal of safety need not (and cannot) ever be fully attained, as long as children know that we adults are actively trying to protect them. This means safety at home, in school, in the immediate environment, and in the world at large.

The second thing that children need is the knowledge that their own efforts can have effects—that they have the potential to act in ways that will be helpful. This can only come from experience in working at those tasks appropriate to their age. In this way they learn that they are not helpless and weak, but that they have "environmental competence," and that their actions can have a positive effect on their environment.

That this is the beginning, and the necessary beginning, of the change to a new morality is clear. What I have been saying here about the needs of children is not farfetched theorizing.

We now know enough about children and how they become adults—to state that these facts are true. Period.

The second step in putting into place any real program in moral education is to realize that one of the central problems is that we usually believe that there is somewhere a method of changing the values of young people in a positive way without changing ourselves. This is a fatal fallacy.

If we are searching for a theory and a curriculum that will improve the development and behavior of students, but not our own, we are on a hopeless quest. Many school administrators and politicians want this. They say, in effect, to the educators, "Teach us how to educate the students in our schools to a better moral development without changing ourselves, the general structure of the schools, the relationships within it, how we ourselves behave, and so forth." This cannot be done.

The educator Lawrence Kohlberg responded to one such request, this one by a school principal, as follows:

> Helping you would mean dealing with real life dilemmas, that is school dilemmas. And dealing with behavior means not only what is just and fair in school dilemmas, but encouraging action to make the school more just. That means trying to promote fairness in teachers behavior as well as in student behavior. So, if you'd like, I'd consider counselling with you and the teachers to make the school a more just community.[1]

The classic studies of Hartshorne and May (1928-1932), and many others since then, have shown that didactic instruction, lecturing about honesty and morality, "character education" classes, had almost no lasting or significant effect on either students' moral judgement or on their moral behavior.

---

[1] L. Kohlberg in Peter Scharf, ed., *Readings in Moral Education* (Oak Grove, MN: Winston Press, 1978), p. 8.

Teaching ethics in the abstract is a dubious procedure at best. We learn an ethical system by acting according to its precepts. Here we learn by doing. The famous story of the philosopher who wanted to learn to swim before he ventured into the water is relevant in this context.

This originally was Hegel's criticism of Kantian philosophy.

The child's learning of right and wrong, an understanding which grows primarily out of the adult-child relationship, but is stabilized in practice with peers.... Children do need the chance to work things out for themselves; they need the struggle, the conflict and the tears to value the pleasures that come with satisfactory solutions....Lecturing is not effective.[2]

Friedrich Froebel, who was largely responsible for originating modern education, stressed two concepts as the basis of what education should strive for. The first was the concept of self-activity (*Selbststätiqkeit*). The second was the concept, in Froebel's language, of *Gleidganzes* which roughly translates into a whole that develops because it is, in turn, part of a larger whole—it is a participant whole.[3]

I share the viewpoint of Susan Blow, a major figure in the development of the kindergarten movement in the United States, that children's learning is essentially social. They:

are understudies in the drama of history. They must learn their lines well before they can, as indeed they properly should, rewrite those lines themselves. Development...is an active interplay between the inner and the outer— the inner and the outer equally valued.[4]

---

[2] Dorothy Cohn, *The Learning Child* (New York: Pantheon, 1972), p. 61.
[3] Friedrich Froebel, *The Education of Man*, W. N. Hailmann, trans. (New York: Augustus M. Kelley, 1974).
[4] Ruth Dropkin and A. Tobier, eds., *Roots of Open Education in America* (New York City: The City College Workshop Center for Open Education, 1976), p. 52.

In this approach you are concerned—like Aristotle—more with the practice than with the theory of morals. From his viewpoint to become a good person, you must behave like a good person. Then you will know what goodness is and be accustomed to living it. This is quite different from the theoretical stance, from Plato to many educational groups in the present, who believed that first there must be the theoretical understanding of ethics, and from this would follow ethical behavior. In Aristotle's words:

> ...a person becomes just by the performance of just actions and temperate by the performance of temperate actions, nor is there the smallest likelihood of a person becoming good by any other course of conduct. This is not, however, a popular line to take, most people preferring theory to practice under the impression that arguing about morals proves them to be philosophers and that in this way they will turn out to be fine characters.[5]

Clearly, of course, both theory and practice are needed. Theory without practice is weak and erratic. Practice without theory is blind action. (See for example, Gordon, Clark and T. V. Smith *Readings in Ethics.*[6])

Between 8 and 11 children begin to be actively concerned with larger questions than those which were central earlier. When 5,000 elementary school children were asked what questions they would like to have answered, their responses included the great moral questions, the ethical problems that philosophers have been asking since far before our records start. And we answer these questions for them by our actions, not our

---

[5] Nichomachean Ethics, Book 2, Chapter 5, in *The Ethics of Aristotle,* J. A. K. Thomson, tr. (London: Penguin, 1955), p. 62.

[6] Published by Appleton-Century-Crofts, New York, 1935, pp. 6 ff.

words. Children follow their adult guides as they actually live, not as they preach.[7]

The educator Philip Jackson invented the term "hidden curriculum" to refer to 90 percent of what goes on in a classroom. We teach far more by example than we do from our textbooks. As long as the hidden curriculum, what one is really taught in a school, includes how to be treated and to act as one of a crowd, how to accept the absolute authority of an appointed stranger, how to work at and learn what one is ordered to from above, how to live and survive in an environment which is concerned with what you do to a school subject and not what the subject does to you, that democratic behavior and individual differences are to be discussed, not lived, that originality and creativity tend to get you into trouble—so long as lessons such as these are the main things taught in our schools—we will not have much improvement in our survival ability. [8]

---

[7] Gertrude Lewis, *Teach Us What We Want to Know* (New York: Mental Health Materials Center, 1969).

[8] The educator Ernest O. Melby has summed this up succinctly when he wrote: "[The present school system] thinks first of what the child must learn and second of the child. We do not measure what school subjects do to the child. We measure what the child does to the school subjects." In F. Raubinger and H. Rowe, eds., *The Individual and Education* (New York: Macmillan, 1968), p. 3. Brackets mine. The usual school system of marking on a curve is a good way of teaching students to compete rather than to cooperate. It has been called "the fang and claw" method of grading. And if you think about the implications to the student of multiple choice tests—such as that originality of thought makes you fail—the concept of the "hidden curriculum" becomes even more clear. In the words of the educator Alice U. Kelliher, "Everything we do in a classroom tells loudly what we care about, what we value...." *Talks with Teachers* (Darien, CT: Educational Publishing Corp., 1958), p. 14.

One day, while working on this book, my phone rang; would I serve on a committee trying to develop methods of teaching ethical behavior to children? My first reaction was, "How do we teach ethics to grownups first?"

But after my initial negative response, I knew that, ethically speaking, I had to try to think about teaching ethics, teaching the meaning of a moral life to children. And I realized that over the past years of thinking about this issue, I had come up with some answers that might be useful.

When my daughter was about eight years old and she saw the Biafran children starving to death on the television screen, she became anxious and fearful. We tried to reassure her, but nothing made any difference until we suggested that she help us raise money, collect canned food and blankets, and join us on a candlelight parade at the U.N. She stopped feeling scared and we observed a new feeling of pride in her.

A social worker in a small town in upstate New York told me that her community was a war zone, overcome by drugs, crime, angry young people, decaying schools. At the opening assembly on the first day of school, a new high school principal (much against his Board's wishes) told the children there would be no classes the first week of school until the community was cleaned up—that no one could concentrate on learning when it looked as if a bomb had fallen on the town. At first the impoverished, deprived kids in high school laughed in glee. This was "Cool!" A time for some more wild and dangerous games. Not so. The classes had to sign in each morning, and, with one or more teachers, were given assignments, such as cleaning the courtyard in front of three buildings, raking, digging, planting pumpkins and other late fall vegetables in a vacant lot (the food to be donated to a "Meals on Wheels" program). They had to pull all the tires and garbage out of the lake in the park, volunteer six hours a day as helpers in a public day care center, a senior citizen's center, or a hospital, under the supervision of the professional staff in each place. A special role for seniors was to answer calls from people asking for specific referral to clinics related to child abuse, drug addiction, and suicide threats.

Most of the people in the community were outraged. How could these kids be responsible? How could they take on jobs for which people need careful training, new skills? A week later, back at the Assembly, there were committees of teachers and children to report. With very few exceptions, everyone had worked hard and done well. The student body voted to continue this work after school, each student would work one day a week, and they would get special credit in social studies.

Wherever and whenever young people have been challenged to be a part of the answer, to join with adults, the results have been spectacular. What it means is that teaching ethics at home or in a classroom has become almost meaningless as our children look at the world today. The answer we can give them is that we understand how hopeless they must feel. We know they feel adults don't truly care about them.

This is a succinct way of making it perfectly clear that children need action and role models; not baseball players who gamble and take drugs, not people who steal—in banks or on the street—not politicians who lie. They need us, their parents and teachers, relatives, friends and neighbors, who do care but often feel too despairing to take action. Taking action can save us as well as our children. The only answer to serious social problems is to do something about them. Of course we have no guarantee it will work, but a basic ethical principle is that you have to keep trying even if you have little hope of winning. When we show concern for our total environment, decency and kindness to each other follows.

This idea is not new, nor is it restricted to the adolescent and above years. Since the 1940s, the City and Country School in New York City has had a "job program." At third grade level, at eight, for example, the children run the school post office which includes a serious job of maintaining all the communications within the school. Out of that they study communication and quite a number of related fields. The social studies arise in part from the tasks that the children actually do in and for their school.

Children in nursery school and kindergarten can bake healthy bran muffins for children who are homeless and living in shelters. Children in the grade school years can give up seeing some of the garbage movies they beg for, and use the money for AIDS research. High school kids can give direct service to others, such as helping to serve meals to the unemployed in a church. Schools can invite elderly people in a nursing home to come see a play, and bring their theater productions to a round of nursing homes and senior centers. Children can develop work teams to help clean up the papers thrown on the ground in a park. Local service agencies nearly all need volunteers. Older children can assist in younger classes. When such programs are developed, the great majority of the children do far better in their schoolwork in a climate of mutual caring and cooperation. And they learn, with and from us, about being part of a community and being part of the human race.

In a growing number of public and high schools, students participate in a project of Amnesty International. They join in one of 3,000 "adoption groups," each of which adopt one or more prisoners who are held unjustly. They write letters to presidents, prison officials, legislators, etc., on behalf of the unjustly imprisoned.

In Bergenfield, New Jersey, high school juniors and seniors staff an aid-to-senior-citizens project. Between 7:30 and 9:30

each morning they telephone elderly people who live alone to see if they are all right. In one year, this resulted in 37 emergency visits to senior citizens by paramedics when there was an emergency that prevented the phone from being answered.[9]

At St. Xavier College in Cincinnati, scholarships are given to two groups—to athletes and to community volunteers who are prepared to work ten hours a week in social agencies, hospitals, etc. Athletes are required to pass all subjects as well. New York University students go to a public park three nights a week as a "watch team." Students patrol the park in groups of four or more with a police officer. Their purpose is to make the park safe for everyone. They must also attend weekly meetings and write a term paper for which they receive regular course credit.

According to the Independent Sector in Washington, a great many students on American campuses are now regularly involved in some form of voluntary social action. The range is very great. It involves programs from free breakfasts for slum children to meals delivered to the elderly, from drug and emergency hotlines to eco-watch organizations, from teaching literacy to ex-convicts to counselling at abortion clinics, from voter registration to law-for-laymen, and to many others. This is indeed "piecemeal engineering" in the best sense of the word. They range widely from promoting social change to short-term and immediate relief, from hands-on programs to theoretical study of community needs.[10]

Experiments on this approach are going on, little by little, all over the Western world, on all levels of education.

At the University of Hacettepe, on the outskirts of Ankara, students registering for the medical school are

_____

[9] These examples were described to me by the educator, Lillian Weber.
[10] For more information, write or call Independent Sector at 1828 L Street, NW, Washington, D.C. 20036, (202) 223-8100.

assigned responsibility for the health of a Turkish family living in a slum area of the city. Throughout their years of study they act as "medical friend" of the family—and in this they have, naturally, the backing of the faculty. When they ultimately receive their degree, much of their knowledge of community medicine has not been learnt from books or lectures; it has been acquired at first hand. Moreover, the development of a sense of social responsibility towards the sick has not been left to chance; it has been built into their course of study from the very first day.[11]

A more advanced project, showing both moral education and incidental learning is described by Sinclair Goodlad in his excellent overview of student social action programs, their problems and advantages, in England:

> As a result of an initiative of this kind, a group of Imperial College engineering undergraduates studied methods of delivering hot food to old people in Hackney [England] during the academic year 1972-3. In 1972-3 the borough of Hackney supplied over 380,000 hot meals to old people who were either housebound or who could walk to their nearest club for a subsidised meal. Some of the food had to meet special dietary requirements, for medical or religious reasons; some was specially prepared for physically or mentally handicapped people. On an average day in Hackney, some 1,500 meals are distributed. The deliveries, which start at 11:30 a.m., have to reach any dwelling in the borough. Great attention is given to ensuring that the meals arrive regularly, for regular visits can be the focal point in the daily routine of old people who are socially isolated....

---

[11] Alec Dickson, "Foreword," in Sinclair Goodlad, *Education and Social Action* (New York: Harper & Row, 1975), p. 8.

> The students' project was to examine the system for
> delivering hot food and see if it could be improved....
> Six students were given a completely free hand to ex-
> amine the existing system and report on it, with sug-
> gestions for improvements....

> Students were able to study the routing of vehicles with
> a computer—learning a new computer language in or-
> der to do so. [12]

The need for moral education has been long known and clearly
recognized. In 1918, The National Education Association of the
United States appointed a special commission to prepare a statement of goals called Purposes of the School. The completed document had as its first and foremost goal: "Provide the child with a
sense of ethics, ethical behavior in human relationships."

Although the need for moral education has been widely
known (even though the way to implement this has not been
clearly understood), fashions do change in education as the
climate of a society changes. The 1918 document was super-
seded by The National Education Association in 1960. The new
commission (headed by the President of Columbia Teachers
College) got right to the point. It began:

> The central purpose of the school is to develop the ratio-
> nal powers of man. The basic subjects for thinking and
> reasoning: English, Mathematics, Science and History. [13]

---

[12] S. Goodlad, *Education and Social Action,* p. 142.

[13] It is far past time to look carefully at our basic attitudes about education—what do we really believe is the purpose of our schools. Unless we
do this, we are not going to make meaningful changes in a system that is
largely failing by almost any standard. In this context, it may be helpful to
recall that the first really heavy Federal money that came to our schools
came, in the United States, after the Russians were the first into space.
First came Sputnik and then the National Defense Education Act. Education was seen as important as it helped in our fight against our enemies.

Fashions change, but the old view of education, that its purpose is "to make the pupils smart and make them good" has generally underlaid educational policy. In the new age in which we are living since Hiroshima, there is a necessary new goal — to develop human beings who can survive and help the race survive in the atomic and space age. Here, as never before, the words of Theodore Roosevelt ring ominously: "To educate a person in mind and not in morals is to educate a menace to society."[14] Or, in more recent parlance, every student who goes through our educational system emerges as either a part of the problem or a part of the solution.[15]

Robert Starrett has distinguished between acts of mercy and acts of justice. In his terms, bringing food to the poor at Christmas is an act of mercy; working to change the social conditions which trap people into poverty is an act of justice. Children may start with acts of mercy, but must be helped by the educational system to go on to acts of justice.[16]

---

[14] Theodore Roosevelt, quoted in Thomas Likona, *Educating for Character* (New York: Bantam, 1991), p. 3.

[15] "It seems to me perfectly clear that we can replace the agenda of the 19th century's pious idealism by something much more exciting—something much more challenging, and certainly not something to be complacent about. We can say that, from here on out, there is going to be one central preoccupation for human beings, for which we must, at all costs, prepare ourselves....that is the task before us of becoming something that we have never really thought much about: becoming the custodians of this planet." David Hawkins, "Developing a New Educational Agenda," in Dropkin and Tobier, *Roots of Open Education in America* (New York City: The City College Workshop Center for Open Education, 1976) p. 57. The emphasis here is on helping children develop relationships with themselves, others, and with the environment. But more is needed in education. Children must also learn skills and content. Herbert Kohl, who understood deeply the importance of human and social growth of the student put it thus: "Teaching does not consist solely of making the youngsters feel good about themselves. It involves helping students gain understanding, knowledge and skills they didn't previously have." *Growing Minds* (New York: Harper & Row, 1984), p. 89.

[16] Robert O. Starrett, *Sowing Seeds of Faith and Justice* (Washington, DC: Jesuit Secondary Education Association Publishers, n.d.), p. 89.

The educator, Dorothy Cohn, has described our present understanding of the development of morality in the child by showing how it begins with the parents' admonitions and examples, and the desire both for parental love and to escape punishment. As the child grows, these are modified by the need to belong to peer groups and to work out the problems of belonging, friendship, and so forth. It is in this actual experience and work that ethical values become a part of the soon-to-be adult. What started as a relationship with adults is solidified, changed, and developed by group activities.

When these include groups with larger goals than their own individual needs, both the person (the individual child) and the social group are helped to develop in healthy and constructive ways. This is what Friedrich Froebel meant by *Gleidganzes*—a whole that develops because it is, in turn, part of a larger whole.

And one may make no mistake about this. By our examples and admonitions, by focusing or not focusing our children's group activities, we do teach a moral code. The only choice we have is what moral code we teach.[17]

Certainly it is true, as many writers have pointed out, that the schools must also teach moral behavior by example—the teacher by caring about these values, the school by acting as if they were important. Thomas Linkona, in his important *Educating for Character*, gives many examples of how this can be done. However, it is necessary to go beyond this. "To develop responsibility, young people need to have responsibility. To learn to care, they must perform caring actions."[18] Many public high schools are now beginning to mandate some form of public service as a graduation requirement. In the face of the increasing

---

[17] Dorothy Cohn, *The Learning Child* (New York: Pantheon, 1972), pp. 2, 3 ff.
[18] Thomas Likona, *Educating for Character* (New York: Bantam, 1991).

demoralization of the ethical climate in the late 20th century, this is progressing faster than is generally realized. The school systems of Atlanta, Detroit, and St. Louis, all sizable cities, now have this requirement with a minimum 75 hours service. An increasing number of schools are affiliating with the Giraffe Project, which gives awards to people who "stick their necks out" by taking unusual action for ethical reasons. Cross-age tutoring and Big-Brother and Big-Sister projects are being developed in ever larger numbers of schools. A list of these and similar programs is given by Fred Newman and Robert Rutter in their "A Profile of High School Community Programs."[19] As there has been a growing recognition by educators that simply knowing right from wrong or having taken verbal courses in ethics is essential, but far from enough, more and more action programs are being instituted. One educator wrote, "We overwhelm children with all the suffering and evil in the world, but do we enable them to act?" More and more this question is being addressed with programs that give children a sense of what Newman has called "environmental competence," the knowledge that they can make a difference, make a real impact on others and on the society in which they live.[20] This can only come about through experiences in which they do make a difference. Newman has made it clear that if children do not learn to act, and take action for the sake of justice and compassion, their verbal learning in this area will have little effect on them or on others. Developing a sense of environmental competence must become a major part and goal of our educational system.

---

[19] Fred Newman and Robert Rutter, "A Profile of High School Community Service Projects," in *Educational Leadership*, December 1985 and January 1986.

[20] Fred W. Newman, *Education for Citizen Action* (Berkeley: McCutchan, 1975).

A good deal of research has shown that one major reason that so little is being done to prevent nuclear war and to protect our failing environment is the belief that individual action can make no real difference—that individuals have no "environmental competence."[21]

And surely children can join us in supporting those organizations that are fighting the good fight against drugs, crime, terrible prison conditions, the proliferation of guns in every classroom, and the poisoning of the planet. One seventh grade teacher told me, "I teach math by fundraising projects for Greenpeace! I teach science by studying what pesticides do to crops. I teach the sacredness of human life by assigning homework which is to watch different TV programs and count the number of killings, or the number of minutes devoted to violence. We write letters to the advertising agencies that sponsor death and destruction. What else is a classroom for?"[22]

I'm sure she spends time on the spelling in those letters, and sees that children add, subtract, multiply, and divide when they figure what it costs to run a Greenpeace or Forever Wild sale, and what the margin of profit will be. When our homes and our classrooms are clearly in the service of improving human life on Earth, our children will become less angry, there will be less feeling of rejection, and in that climate learning can take place.

Of course we need to point to all the good people who care and live righteous lives, but the message will be lost until we say to our children, "Help us to change the world." Ethics begins with that message.[23]

---

[21] Kenneth Field and John A. Kevin, "Why Doesn't Everyone Work to Prevent Nuclear War?" in *Journal of Applied Psychology*, 1988, Vol. 18, No. 1, pp. 59-65.

[22] From personal communication with Helen Strauss, 1992.

[23] For a fuller discussion of concepts in this chapter, see Eda J. LeShan, *The Conspiracy Against Childhood* (New York: Atheneum, 1976).

This, of course, is far from the full answer needed to change the ethical climate in the world in the late 20th century. As I have tried to illustrate, we need much more. It is, however, a step we can take, and is the kind of step that has proven itself of real value and is practical. It is "piecemeal engineering" rather than "Utopian engineering." It is the kind of approach that sets an example and a model for our children. The old Chinese proverb asks how one sets out on the longest journey in the world. The answer is, "By putting out the left foot."

In no way does this approach rule out such methods of teaching ethical behavior as the cognitive-developmental methodology developed by Lawrence Kohlberg. These can only be an aid as they help teach children how to think about moral problems. However, they are far from enough. Much deeper changes—a change in the foundation of our entire conceptualizing—will be necessary if we wish to survive.

The suggestions here are only a small beginning. They indicate some of the directions we need to take if we wish to lead our children to an ethical viewpoint that will help them survive the atomic and space age.

It will not be easy. The examples of change are of the kind of activities that are going on in only a very small percentage of our educational institutions. Seymour Sarason, in his important book, *The Culture of the School and the Problem of Change*, has shown how difficult real change is in the schools. For reasons that Sarason describes in detail, there is a tremendous problem of inertia, and a strong tendency to return to old patterns of "behavioral regularities" (patterns of recurrent behavior) in our educational systems.[24] Putting any new methods into place is like swimming upstream in a rapidly flowing

---

[24] Seymour Sarason, *The Culture of the School and the Problem of Change* (Boston: Alleyn and Bacon, 1971).

river. As soon as one stops swimming, one is swept back to where one started from.

But, difficult or not, we must change. Eleanor Roosevelt once put it, "The whole future of our country depends on the education of our children."[25] It is now more than that. The whole future of our species depends on it.

---

[25] A. Kelliher, *Talks with Teachers* (Darien, CT: Educational Publishing Corp., 1958), p. 3.

BIBLIOGRAPHY

Abel, R. *Man is the Measure*. New York: Free Press, 1976.

Arendt, Hannah. *Eichmann in Jerusalem*. New York: Viking, 1963.

Aristotle. *The Ethics of Aristotle*. J. A. K. Thomson, tr. London: Penguin, 1955.

Beard, Charles. *Whither Mankind*. New York: Lomgamns-Green, 1928 .

Berger, Peter and H. Kellner. *The Homeless Mind*. New York: Vintage-Random House, 1973.

Berlin, Isaiah. *The Crooked Timber of Humanity*. New York: Knopf, 1991.

———. *Against the Current*. New York: Penguin, 1971.

Bevington, H. *Beautiful and Lofty People*. New York: Harcourt Brace Jovanovitch, 1946 .

Bridges, H. J. *Aspects of Ethical Religion*. New York: American Ethical Union, 1926 .

Cahn, Edmund. *The Moral Decision*. Bloomington, IN: Indiana University Press, 1955.

———. *The Sense of Injustice*. London: Oxford University Press, 1949.

Cantor, Norman and Michael Wertheimer. *The Making of the Modern World, 1815-1914*. New York: Thomas Crowell, 1967.

Chipp, H. B. *Theories of Modern Art*. Berkeley: University of California Press, 1956.

Clark, Gordon and T. V. Smith. *Readings in Ethics*. New York: Appleton-Century-Crofts, 1935.

Cohen, Morris Raphael. *Reason and Nature*. New York: Harcourt Brace & Co., 1931.

Cohn, Dorothy. *The Learning Child*. New York: Pantheon, 1972.

Corwin, Norman. *Overkill and Megalove*. New York: World Publ. Co., 1963.

Dewey, John. *Human Nature and Conduct*. New York: Modern Library, 1930.

———. *Reconstruction in Philosophy*. Boston: Beacon Press, 1948.

Disch, Robert, ed. *The Ecological Conscience*. Englewood Cliffs, N. J.: Prentice-Hall, 1970 .

Dropkin, Ruth and A. Tobier, eds. *Roots of Open Education in America*. New York City: The City College Workshop Center for Open Education, 1976 .

Dubler, Nancy and Davin Nimmons. *Ethics on Call*. New York: Crown-Harmony, 1992.

Erlich, Paul R. and Anne H. Erlich. *The Population Explosion*. New York: Simon & Schuster, 1990.

Freud, Sigmund. *Civilization and its Discontents*. New York: W. W. Norton & Co ., 1962 .

Friedenberg, Edgar Z. *The Vanishing Adolescent*. New York: Dell Paperback, 1962.

Froebel, Freiedrich. *The Education of Man*. W.N. Hailmann, trans. New York: Augustus M. Kelley, 1974.

Geertz, C. R. *The Interpretation of Cultures*. New York: Basic Books, 1973.

Goodlad, Sinclair. *Education and Social Action*. New York: Harper & Row, 1975.

Guderian, Heinz. *Panzer Leader*. New York: Ballantine, 1952.

Hall, E. T. *Beyond Culture*. New York: Doubleday, 1971.

Heggenhoughen, Kris. *The Naked Anthropologist: Tales from Around the World*. Philip R. DeVita, ed. New York: Wadsworth, 1991.

Hofstadter, Richard. *Social Darwinism in American Thought*. New York: George Braziller, 1969.

James, William. *Approaches to Ethics*. New York: McGraw-Hill, 1962.

———. *A Pluralistic Universe*. Cambridge: Cambridge University Press, 1977.

Jones, W. T., et al, eds. *Approaches to Ethics*. New York: McGraw Hill, 1962.

Jung, Robert K. *Brighter Than a Thousand Suns*. New York: Harcourt Brace, 1950.

Kelliher, Alice U. *Talks with Teachers*. Darien, CT: Educational Publishing Corp., 1958.

Kennedy, Edward M. and Mark O. Hatfield. *Freeze! How You Can Help Prevent Nuclear War*. New York: Bantam, 1982.

Koestler, Arthur. *Janus*. New York: Random House, 1978.

———. *Thieves in the Night*. New York: Macmillan, 1946.

———. *The Trail of the Dinosaur*. New York: MacMillan, 1955.

Kohl, Herbert. *Growing Minds*. New York: Harper & Row, 1984.

LeShan, Eda. *The Conspiracy Against Childhood*. New York: Antheneum, 1968.

LeShan, L. *The Dilemma of Psychology: A Psychologist Looks at His Troubled Profession*. New York: Dutton, 1990.

———. *The Psychology of War*. Chicago: Noble, 1992.

LeShan, L. and Henry Margenau. *Einstein's Space and Van Gogh's Sky*. New York: MacMillan, 1982.

Lessing, Gotthold E. *Nathan the Wise*. Bayard Morgan, tr. New York: Frederic Ungar Publ., 1955.

Lewis, Gertrude. *Teach Us What We Want to Know*. New York: Mental Health Materials Center, 1969.

Likona, Thomas. *Educating for Character*. New York: Bantam, 1991.

Lorenz, Konrad. *The Waning of Humanness*. Boston: Little Brown, 1983.

Michalson, Gordon E. *Fallen Freedom*. Cambridge: Cambridge University Press, 1990.

Midgley, Mary. *Can't We Make Moral Judgements?* New York: St. Martin's Press, 1991.

Mill, John S. *On Liberty*. New York: Penguin, 1974.

Montesquieu. *Les Philosophes*. Norman Torrey, ed. New York: Capricorn Books, 1960.

Mothershead, John L. *Ethics*. New York: Holt, Rinehart, Winston, 1955.

Mumford, Lewis. *The Conduct of Life*. New York: Harcourt Brace, 1951.

———. *The Transformations of Man*. New York: Harper, 1956.

Newman, Fred W. *Education for Citizen Action*. Berkeley: McCutchan, 1975.

Newman, Fred and Robert Rutter. "A Profile of High School Community Service Projects." *Educational Leadership* (Dec. 1985 and Jan. 1986).

Otto, Max. *Science and the Moral Life*. New York: Mentor-NAL, 1949.

Pascal, Blaise. *Pensées*. London: J. M. Dent, 1932.

Popper, Karl R. *The Open Society and Its Enemies*, Vol. I. Princeton, NJ: Princeton University Press, 1966.

Raubinger, Frederick and Harold Rowe. *The Individual and Education*. New York: Macmillan, 1968.

Salvadori, Mario. "Fermi's Nuclear Policies." *The Sciences* (March-April 1992).

Sarason, Seymour. *The Culture of the School and the Problem of Change*. Boston: Alleyn and Bacon, 1971.

Scharf, Peter, ed. *Readings in Moral Education*. Oak Grove, MN: Winston Press, 1978.

Schell, Jonathan. *The Fate of the Earth*. New York: Knopf, 1982.

Schweitzer, Albert. "The Problem of Ethics for Twentieth-Century Man." *The Saturday Review of Literature* (13 June 1953).

Starrett, Robert O. *Sowing Seeds of Faith and Justice*. Washington, DC: Jesuit Secondary Education Association Publishers, n.d.

Szent-Gyorgyi, Albert. *The Crazy Ape*. New York: Philosophical Library, 1970.

Tyrrell, G. N. M. *Grades of Significance*. London: Rider & Co., 1930.

Viney, Wayne. "The Cyclops and the Twelve-Eyed Toad." *American Psychologist*, Vol. 44, No. 10 (Oct. 1989).

Warren, Earl G. "The Law Beyond the Law." *Main Currents in Modern Thought*, Retrospective Issue, Vol. 32 (Nov. 17, 1975).

Whitehead, Alfred North. *Religion in the Making*. New York: Macmillan, 1926.